*Aural Images
of Lost Traditions*

ROBERT TOFT

AURAL IMAGES OF LOST TRADITIONS

Sharps and Flats in the Sixteenth Century

University of Toronto Press
TORONTO BUFFALO LONDON

University of Toronto Press 1992
Toronto Buffalo London
Printed in Canada
ISBN 0-8020-5929-5

Printed on acid-free paper

Canadian Cataloguing in Publication Data

Toft, Robert
Aural images of lost traditions

Includes bibliographical references and index.
ISBN 0-8020-5929-5

1. Musical pitch.   2. Vocal music – 16th century –
History and criticism.   3. Music – 16th century –
History and criticism.   I. Title.

This book has been published with the help of a grant from the Canadian Federa-
tion for the Humanities, using funds provided by the Social Sciences and
Humanities Research Council of Canada.

CONTENTS

ACKNOWLEDGMENTS

I wish to express my gratitude to all those who aided in the development of this study: to Reinhard Strohm, Brian Trowell, and Howard Brown for reading earlier versions of the book and for their advice and useful suggestions; to Cynthia Leive, Music Librarian at McGill University, and her staff for creating a microfilm archive of sixteenth-century music sources and for many kindnesses; to Herbert Kellman and Jerry Call for placing the University of Illinois Musicological Archives for Renaissance Manuscript Studies at my disposal and for answering my queries; to Charles Jacobs for providing photocopies of his MA thesis; to Arthur Ness for preparing a list of variants in Francesco da Milano's tablature sources; to Horst Loeschmann for his generous help in collecting variants in motet sources; and to James Grier, Joseph Schmidt, and Monica Harvey for advice on the translations. Any errors, omissions, or misinterpretations of the material used in this study remain, of course, my own responsibility.

I never would have been able to undertake the research for this book if it had not been for the financial support of the Social Sciences and Humanities Research Council of Canada through two fellowships which enabled me to work at the British Library and the Cambridge

University Library for three years. I am particularly grateful to the staff of the British Library for their efficient and courteous help while I spent a year transcribing and editing sixteenth-century tablatures. To the Faculties of Graduate Studies at McGill University and the University of Western Ontario, I extend my gratitude for various grants which facilitated the production of this book.

Portions of Chapter 4 originally appeared in 'Pitch Content and Modal Procedure in Josquin's *Absalon, fili mi*,' TVNM 33 (1983) 3–27 and 'Traditions of Pitch Content in the Sources of Two Sixteenth-Century Motets,' ML 69 (1988) 334–44 (by permission of Oxford University Press).

And finally, this project never would have been completed without the constant support and encouragement of my family.

Aural Images of Lost Traditions

INTRODUCTION

One of the major problems confronting the performer of Renaissance vocal music has been to establish a precise understanding of the traditions of pitch-content associated with specific compositions. Performers and scholars working toward this end – the recovery of the actual pitches implied by mensural notation – have long been plagued by the ambiguities of pitch notation in the sources of vocal music from this period. The signs *b mollis* and *b durum* (flat and sharp) were largely left unspecified in vocal sources; consequently, certain important details of composers' intentions never were notated. Singers were expected to be familiar with the principles governing the application of these signs and to make the appropriate alterations at the time of performance; the final shaping of the music in both harmonic and melodic content was their responsibility. Although these principles were discussed in contemporary theoretical treatises and manuals, the explanations are far too cursory to allow us to reconstruct fully the oral traditions which sixteenth-century vocal notation only partly records. Throughout this century, however, keyboard players, lutenists, vihuelists, and guitarists continually intabulated vocal music for their respective instruments. These transcriptions have recorded the practices of many of the greatest performers of the era, providing modern performers and scholars with a precise view of how sixteenth-century musicians added sharps and flats to the vocal sources with which they worked.

We are, in essence, dealing with three transmissions of the same information. Two of them, theoretical writings and vocal sources, even when used together, present an incomplete picture: vocal sources, for the most part, lack notated sharps and flats, and theorists explain how to incorporate unspecified signs in too general a fashion. Fortunately, tablatures tell us exactly what notes individual musicians performed. The very act of translating vocal notation into letter notation requires the intabulator to make implicit solmization practices explicit. In reality, letters are simply the tablature equivalents of notes and are just another way of schematically representing the pitch to be performed. Tablatures, then, help to create as 'thick' a context as possible for a discussion of sharps and flats. To concentrate solely on any one of the three kinds of documents would isolate a single strand of a three-part complex from the other two related parts, and this would create too 'thin' a context for one to draw significant conclusions.[1] Therefore, an examination of intabulations, coupled with a reconstruction of the theoretical framework surrounding the incorporation of *b mollis* and *b durum*, is essential if we are to ascertain fully the details of pitch-content and modal procedure operative in vocal sources during the period. The study of tablatures demonstrates that more than one way of solmizing specific passages existed among performers in the sixteenth century, and intabulations document the range of practices that were known. To force one method of solmization on to all sixteenth-century musicians, whether they were German or Italian or lived at the beginning, middle, or end of the century, would distort our perception of the period. The variety of practices exhibited in intabulations does not necessarily reveal that instrumentalists lacked a consistent approach to their art; instead, it illustrates the different ways in which theoretical precepts and conventions could be applied.

In any reconstruction of a past tradition, it is necessary to determine the boundaries of the style. This must be achieved not only by documenting the range of theoretical possibilities that was open to the performer but also by indicating which sharps and flats practising musicians actually incorporated in their performances. The interaction of these two avenues of approach should produce a reasonably accurate picture of contemporary performing practices. I will demonstrate that both singers and instrumentalists worked within the theoretical framework that survives in late fifteenth- and in sixteenth-century treatises and that the precepts and conventions discussed in these treatises were by no means immutable. The recognition of the existence of a range of practices will considerably modify our understanding of modal polyphony. The lack of systematic knowledge in this area has forced modern editors and performers to base their own interpretations of pitch-content on incomplete documentary evidence. This book attempts to establish the parameters of sixteenth-century practices and to present guide-lines for modern performers and scholars. Specific practices are discussed in Chapter 3 ('The German Custom') and Chapter 4 ('Traditions of Pitch-Content'), whereas the focus of Chapter 1 ('Theoretical Framework') and Chapter 2 ('Pitch-Content in Josquin's Motets') is deliberately broad and reveals the wide range of practices that were known throughout Europe in the sixteenth century. With the exception of Germany, it has proved impossible to detect national and chronological trends, as elements of conservatism and radicalism coexisted throughout the century. The view that the use of sharps and flats changed dramatically from decade to decade or from country to country is not supported by intabulations. In fact, the use of *b mollis* and *b durum* in the intabulations of Josquin's motets is frequently identical for musicians who lived in Italy in 1507, Germany in 1533, France in 1547, and Spain in 1578, regardless of whether the intabulation was for lute, vihuela, or keyboard.

The study begins with a discussion of the theoretical framework surrounding the incorporation of *b mollis* and *b durum*. In reconstructing this framework, I allow the theorists to speak for themselves, and I include, therefore, frequent direct quotations from treatises. Rather than search for definitive statements which can be moulded into a convenient group of rules applicable to all situations, the first chapter emphasizes the inherent flexibility that actually pervaded theorists' remarks. The following chapters, which centre on practical sources, determine the frequency with which advice from theorists was followed and demonstrate which exceptions to theoretical precepts were common. All of the practices encountered in the intabulations are rooted in the theoretical tradition of the period, and discussing both theoretical and practical sources under one cover makes it possible to forge a link between vocal music and instrumental intabulations of vocal works.

Chapter 2 considers a composer whose music repeatedly was chosen for intabulation in the sixteenth century – Josquin Desprez (d 1521). A number of Josquin's motets were intabulated during that century, and fifteen of these works have been chosen as the subject for this chapter. The motets were selected in preference to Josquin's mass cycles or to his secular works because the extant sources for both the intabulations and the motets themselves span the longest time period (the printed intabulations are dated between 1507 and 1578 and the printed vocal sources between 1504 and 1616) and encompass the widest geographic area (Poland, Germany, France, Spain, and Italy), and therefore offer a substantial cross-section of sixteenth-century practices. Although this chapter does not purport to explain what Josquin's own practices might have been,[2] it does illustrate how musicians during the sixty years after his death interpreted the pitch-content of his motets. Compositional style changed dramatically in this period, yet Josquin's music persisted in the repertory of church choirs for many decades (as the number of times it was published or copied into manuscripts shows) and thus provides us with a stable, living body of music in which we can investigate the use of sharps and flats throughout almost the entire century.

Chapter 3 investigates the nationalistic German practices discussed in the middle of the sixteenth century by the brothers Paul and Bartholomeus Hessen and documents those practices in German tablature sources, particularly in the tablatures of Hans Gerle. The final chapter reveals the various traditions of pitch-content associated with five works: Josquin's 'Inviolata, integra et casta es' and 'Pater noster,' a setting of 'Absalon, fili mi' which may or may not have been composed by Josquin, Clemens non Papa's 'Fremuit spiritu Jesus,' and Alexander Agricola's 'Si dedero.'

The research builds upon the work of others who have trod before me on this most controversial ground. Articles by Willi Apel, Jaap van Bentham, James Haar, and Thomas Noblitt have shown that nonharmonic (false) relations were a characteristic feature of sixteenth-century vocal music, and the broad spectrum of intabulations examined in this book confirms these writers' findings. In addition, a number of scholars have demonstrated the importance of using tablatures to document pitch-content in vocal music, and I am indebted to them for their work. Most important, it was Howard M. Brown's studies on plucked-instrument intabulations which revealed the potential that this vast untapped repertoire provided for documenting the practices discussed in this book. Nonetheless, many scholars and performers are reluctant to recognize the value of intabulations, and one of my main purposes in writing this book is to challenge them to rethink their position. It is my belief that our modern view of the use of sharps and flats in vocal music has been far too narrow. Much more daring practices, especially with regard to dissonance treatment, were the norm in the sixteenth century, and slowly this fact is being recognized.

I was delighted to read Karol Berger's valuable new book on the theoretical literature dealing with *musica ficta* at a point when I was completing this book. My own work on theoretical sources dates back to 1983, when I first reported on the problem in my PHD dissertation, and I am particularly pleased to see that in one respect our approach is somewhat similar, that is, that we both emphasize the flexibility with which theorists treated the subject. My book expands on Berger's work by focusing on practical sources, by including discussions from theorists writing after 1558 (the terminal date for Berger's study), and by highlighting some of Juan Bermudo's most illuminating remarks on the use of sharps and flats – an author largely untapped by Berger. A study as comprehensive as Berger's deserves comment, and I have indicated where my views agree with his and where they conflict. Most of my comments appear in the notes and relate mainly to his sections on the method of correcting vertical and horizontal problems, for this is where tablatures really can finely tune the theoretical literature.

Throughout my study, books, articles, editions, and manuscripts will be cited in an abbreviated form. For example, the reference 'Apel *Punto*' is an abbreviation of 'Willi Apel, "Punto intenso contra remisso," in *Music East and West* ed Thomas Noblitt (New York 1981) 175–82,' and the reference 'Bermudo *Dec* IV 48, f 87v' is a shortened form of 'Juan Bermudo, *Declaración de instrumentos musicales* (Osuna 1555) IV chap 48, f 87v.' Similarly, 'Brussels 215–16' designates the source 'Brussels, Bibliothèque Royale, mss 215–16.' Printed tablature sources are cited by their numbers in Howard M. Brown's *Instrumental Music Printed before 1600: A Bibliography* (Cambridge, Mass 1965), and printed vocal sources are cited by their RISM number. The spelling of titles of early books follows RISM and/or Brown. All abbreviations are listed in the Bibliography.

As much as possible, I have tried to avoid anachronistic musical terminology, preferring to derive terms from Renaissance theoretical literature. The book employs, therefore, a number of terms which are not in common use, and definitions appear in the Glossary. Please consult any of the standard reference works, such as the *New Grove*, when fuller explanations are required. Unless stated otherwise, all translations are my own. Transcriptions of many of the intabulations used in this study can be found in Toft *Pitch* vol 2.

ONE

Theoretical Framework

The theoretical guide-lines governing the sixteenth-century musician's approach to the application of the signs *b mollis* and *b durum* survive in a number of treatises dating from the late fifteenth to the early seventeenth centuries. Unfortunately, no one author treats the subject exhaustively or codifies the precepts, and if the parameters of the practices are to be established, isolated statements must be gleaned from treatises written throughout this period. These treatises deal with a variety of subjects and styles of music, and although most of them do not date from Josquin's lifetime (the main composer treated in this book), many of them are contemporaneous with both the vocal sources of his motets and the intabulations of those sources. In fact, the information contained in the treatises regarding the use of sharps and flats, treatment of dissonance, and so on is consistent with the practices exhibited in the intabulations. My discussion centres on those treatises which date from the same time period as the intabulations, that is, 1530–60, the study being expanded to include theorists as early as Tinctoris (1476 and 1477) and as late as Correa (1626) when these theorists illuminate practices encountered in the intabulations. Correa, for example, specifically addresses the music of Josquin and Gombert and provides the only discussion known to me which clearly explains the use of simultaneous dissonant octaves in the sixteenth century. I have included a great deal of material from those theorists who direct their writings to instrumentalists. Both Juan Bermudo (1555) and Tomás de Sancta Maria (1565) address keyboard players and vihuelists, and their treatises show that instrumentalists learned the same theoretical principles as singers. Furthermore, the focus of the chapter is deliberately broad, for my purpose is to present the range of theoretical options that was open to performers of the period.

The sections of the treatises in which the relevant discussions are found are quite diverse. The comments frequently are embedded in passages which treat various aspects of the art of counterpoint, but similar remarks also are found in sections devoted to solmization, modes, *musica ficta*, the semichromatic genus, and the function of sharps and flats.[1] It would appear, then, that theorists never considered the issue of how to incorporate sharps and flats in vocal music as a topic in its own right, that is, as a subject which should receive separate treatment. Many of the most informative discussions occur in the form of advice to composers on the ways of structuring counterpoint properly so that the desired results would be produced in performance. In other words, theorists seem to imply that composers should write their counterpoint clearly and that their doing so would enable singers to know when to add sharps and flats. Perhaps we are dealing with two distinct but closely related areas: theoretical principles and the practical application of those principles. Treatises establish the general guidelines for using sharps and flats but do little to clarify specific practical applications, presumably because the addition of *b mollis* and *b durum* to vocal music was the concern more of performers than of theorists.[2]

As one would expect, the comments in the treatises directed to the use of sharps and flats occasionally present conflicting viewpoints, and no consensus exists either in the treatises or, as will be shown in the next chapter, in the approaches taken by performers. So rather than take isolated statements which on the surface appear to be definitive and artificially create from them a single set of rules to govern all sixteenth-century music, this chapter will stress the inherent flexibility which actually pervaded the theorists' remarks. Apparently, these comments applied to instrumentalists as well as singers, for I have found no evidence which suggests that a separate theoretical system existed for instrumentalists. Indeed, two theorists specifically state that their remarks govern both groups of musicians. Juan Bermudo (1555) and Tomás de Sancta Maria (1565) make this clear. At several points in his treatise, Bermudo asserts that his discussion of theoretical principles pertains to either singing or playing.[3] Later in the century, Sancta Maria echoes Bermudo's contention by asserting that 'what is unsingable may not be played.'[4] Since theorists did not differentiate between singers and players, the precepts outlined in their treatises have a direct bearing on the practices encountered in the intabulations and therefore will form the basis for an explanation of the instrumentalists' procedures.

Any sixteenth-century performer who had worked with contemporary vocal sources would have been familiar with the notational ambiguities that permeated the vast majority of manuscripts and printed books. Many of the required sharps and flats were not specified in these vocal sources, and the final shaping of the music was left to the performer. As a result, certain melodic details rarely were notated. However, some theorists, such as Stephano Vanneo (1533), regarded the specification of these details as unnecessary: 'Diesis figura quae ad rudium tantum noticiam (quibus numquam satis fit) subscribi solet' / 'The sharp sign is usually written down only for the edification of the unskilled (who are never satisfied)' (Vanneo *RMA* III 36, f 90r).

Numerous matters, such as the removal of vertical and melodic dissonance, were left for the performer to resolve. In fact, one theorist, Johannes Tinctoris (1476), considered the avoidance of the melodic tritone in *tritus* modes to be such a matter of routine that the mandatory sign did not need to be notated: 'Neque tunc bmollis signum apponi est necessarium, immo si appositum videatur, asininum esse dicitur' / 'Nor then is it necessary to mark the sign *bmollis* [to remove the tritone]; rather, if it is seen to have been marked, it is said to be asinine' (Tinctoris *NPT* 8, p 74).

Yet not all writers shared the view expressed by Vanneo and Tinctoris that composers could rely on performers to supply correctly information missing from vocal sources. Several theorists, recognizing the inadequacy of contemporary notational practices, called for composers to mark their intentions fully. Pietro Aaron, in the *Aggiunta*

to his *Toscanello* (1529), states the position most clearly: 'Hora si ris-
ponde se il cantore è ubbligato overamente puo cantando uno canto
non da lui piu visto cognoscere, o intendere l'intento & secreto del
compositore da lui piu pensato al primo moto, si conclude che no: se
bene suffi quello che celebro la musica benche alcuni il contrario
pensono' / 'We will now consider whether the singer is obliged to
or is truly able to sing a song from sight or understand at once
the intentions and secrets of the composer. We conclude that the
answer is no, although among the wise men who celebrate music
some think the contrary' (Aaron *ToscA* f Niiv). He later expands his
discussion of the sign *b mollis* by comparing the problems of ambiguous notation to the signposts encountered by the traveller:

> Et piu si vede in alcuni viaggi dove si truovono varii segnali, &
> questo per essergli piu strade da potere caminare: onde acio che
> quegli che non fanno per quel paese andare, possino rettamente
> pigliare il buon camino dove non essendo segno alcuno, senza
> dubbio potrebbono pigliare la cativa via ... Pertanto il Musico
> overo Compositore è ubbligato segnare lo intento suo: acio che
> il cantore non incorra in quello che dal detto compositore non
> fu mai pensato. Concludo adunque come ho detto, che tal
> segno é cosi conveniente a gli dotti, come a gli indotti: & dico
> che il cantore non é tenuto nel primo moto, cantare le note ne
> gli luoghi dove tal segno puo accadere, se tal segno non appare:
> perche potrebbe errare ... Et questo si intende ne gli concenti
> non provisti: cioe non prima cantati, overamente considerati /
> And furthermore we see that in some journeys one may find
> various signs because there are several roads one could take.
> Therefore, whether or not one knows the countryside through
> which one is going, [the signs] would be placed correctly to
> show the right way. Where there is no sign, some, no doubt,
> might take the wrong road ... Consequently, the musician or
> composer is obliged to mark his intention so that the singer will
> not fall into something that the composer did not intend. I
> conclude, then, as I have said, that such a sign is as useful to the
> experienced as to the inexperienced. And I say that because one
> might err the singer is not expected to sing at first sight the

[correct] notes in the places where such a sign might occur, [especially] if such a sign does not appear ... And this we understand in songs that are not rehearsed, that is, not sung before or truly examined. (Aaron *ToscA* f Niiiv–Nivr)

As late as 1619, theorists were still imploring composers to notate precisely all of the sharps and flats required by the music: 'Darumb denn die beste Caution wehre / wenn es die Componisten in allen örten; Da es von nöthen ist / klärlich darbey schrieben / so hette man keines nach sinnens oder zweiffels von nöthen' / 'Therefore, the best precaution would be for composers to notate them [diese beyde Signa Chromatica] clearly in all the places where they are necessary, so that there would be little speculation or doubt about their necessity' (Praetorius *SM* III 3, p 31).

Nevertheless, even if vocal sources contained all of the necessary sharps and flats, our understanding of the Renaissance use of these signs is imperfect. For example, we do not know exactly how they affect hexachord transposition or the solmization of individual voices. Nor do we know if these signs indicate that specific notes should be raised or lowered, as certain theorists suggest, or if they affect an entire hexachord, as others maintain. Nor do we fully comprehend the relationship between signatures and the signs that appear within a work. In short, it is impossible to determine with complete confidence which practices are embodied in any given scribe's notational conventions.

However, in spite of these difficulties, many of the statements made by theorists concerning *b mollis* and *b durum* do shed light on one of the conventions associated with these signs. Adrian Le Roy (1574) states that 'b sharpe doeth holde up the tune halfe a note higher, and b flatte, contrarywise doeth lette it fall halfe a note lower.'[5] And Giovanni Spataro (1524), Giovanni Maria Lanfranco (1533), and Gioseffo Zarlino (1558) implied the same by maintaining that the signs *b mollis* and *b durum* caused the removal or the addition of a semitone:[6]

il primo .S.♯ remove el sono naturale per Semitonio maggiore in acuto: el secondo .S. b opera per contrario; S. che remove el sono dal loco naturale per Semitonio maggiore in grave / the first sign ♯ removes the natural sound a major semitone higher.

The second sign *b* works in the opposite way in that it removes the sound from the natural place a major semitone lower. (Spataro quoted in Artusi *L'Artusi* f 23v)

il segno del Diesis: & quello del b, molle (cosi nominati da i prattici) fanno un medesimo effetto: ma per contrario moto: Conciosiacosa chel loro oprar non sia altro: chel torre: & dare a gli intervalli: il Semituon maggiore da gli antichi chiamato Apotome / the sign of the *diesis* and that of *b molle* (so named by the practitioners) cause a similar effect but by contrary motion; indeed their work [is] none other than removing and giving to the intervals the major semitone called by the ancients 'Apotome.' (Lanfranco *SM* IV, p 125)

Gli effetti adunque delle dette cifere, o segni [♮, ♭, and ♯] ... è di aggiungere, o di levare il Semituono minore dal Tuono ... / The effects, then, of these ciphers or signs [♮, ♭, and ♯] ... is to add or to subtract the small semitone from a tone. (Zarlino *IH* III 25, p 170)

Although these descriptions of the function of sharps and flats seem clear enough, the jurisdiction of each sign that appears within a piece is not always obvious, and many of the statements by theorists regarding the signs *b mollis* and *b durum* do little to clarify individual problems. Ornithoparchus' (1517) comment on the matter is vague: 'As often as *fa* or *mi* is marked contrary to their nature [that is, when a sign is placed where it would not normally occur], the *Solfaer* must follow the marke so long as it lasts.'[7] And even though Tinctoris (1476) differentiates between a sign that is used as a signature and one that is used within a piece, he does not state explicitly how long a *deductio* which contains the sign *b mollis* remains in effect: 'quodsi [signum bmollis] in exordio linearum ponatur, totus cantus per b molle cantabitur. Si vero in quavis alia parte positum sit, quam diu deductio cui praeponetur durabit, tam diu cantus b mollaris erit' / 'but if [the sign *b mollis*] is placed at the beginning of the line, the whole *cantus* will be sung with *b mollis*. If, however, it is placed in any other location, the *cantus* will be sung with *b mollis* for as long as the *deductio* in which it is prefaced lasts' (Tinctoris

NPT 8, p 74). Lanfranco (1533), on the other hand, more narrowly defines the role of the sign *b mollis*: 'che in ogni luogo de ♮.quadro: dove si trova il .b. rotondo: che alla nota di quel b. si dica: fa: ritonando subito allordine di ♮.quadro: percioche il detto b.molle si interpone nellordine di ♮.quadro per far consonanza, & non per rompere lordine principale' / 'in every place of ♮*quadro* [that is, the scale of *b durum* (pieces with no signature)] where one finds the *b rotondo*, on the note of this *b* one says *fa* returning immediately to the order of ♮*quadro*, since the said *b molle* is inserted in the order of ♮*quadro* to make consonance and not to interrupt the principal order' (Lanfranco *SM* I, p 18). His remarks on the limited jurisdiction of the sign *b mollis* are corroborated by Hans Gerle (1546): 'Nun werden meer fa in dem gesang gemacht / wie ich daforn auch anzengt hab / die selben stehen im gesang dinnen / unnd nicht zu forderst / dasselbig fa wo es im Gesang stehet / gehört es nur zu der Noten die gerichts nach dem fa folget / und nit zu den andern noten / dann so baldt die selb not auss ist so geet das fa die andern Noten / die eben auff der lini oder in den spacii stehen nichts meer an / Es werd dann auch ein fa für ein n[o]tliche geschriben' / 'Now more *fas* [flats] are used in song. As I have indicated before, these *fas* are located within song and not at the beginning. When these *fas* are located within song, they belong only to the notes which follow right after the *fas* and not to the other notes. For as soon as the same note has ended, the *fa* no longer affects the other notes on that line or in that space. One would write, then, a *fa* for each note[8] (Gerle *MT* f b2v). But despite Gerle's unequivocal description of the practices surrounding flats, few of the vocal sources that survive from his lifetime (ca 1500–70) are as specific as he imagines them to be. Typically, mensural sources merely outline pitch-content, because most of the required sharps and flats had to be supplied by the performer.

But what theoretical principles guided the performer, and how are these precepts discussed during the period under consideration? The information collected from the various treatises has generated four main areas to be considered – the treatment of *clausulae* and related figures, vertical dissonance, melodic dissonance, and mimetic passages. This organization of the material represents a modern reconstruction of the theoretical framework that would have been accessible to the sixteenth-century musician.

Treatment of Clausulae *and Related Figures*

Ornithoparchus, citing Tinctoris as his authority, defined a *clausula* as a phrase which ends in either rest or perfection, or the conjunction of the various voices in perfect concords.[9] This basic definition was known throughout the century, and by the mid-1500s, certain theorists, such as Gioseffo Zarlino (1558), provided a more elaborate discussion of the term.[10] Zarlino equated *cadenze* to the punctuation used in writing and oratory, borrowing grammatical terms to describe the various types of cadences employed in musical composition. He defined the cadence as a certain action that the voices perform together which denotes either a general repose of the harmony or the perfection of the sense of the words upon which the piece is composed. He expanded this definition by stating that the cadence is a certain termination of one part of a larger composition at a midpoint, at a distinction of the argument of the oration, or at a final termination. The cadence, he maintained, is equivalent to the *punto* (that is, punctuation) of an oration and could be called the *punto* of musical composition. Zarlino equated these resting points to the pauses one makes in the argument of an oration, not only at a middle distinction but also at a final one.

In conclusion, he stated that cadences were invented for designating the perfection of the parts of a larger composition and for marking the ends of perfect sentences of the text. In these latter places, one should use an absolute or perfect cadence on an octave or unison (see Ex 1.1). But for the middle distinctions of the harmony and the text, that is, when the sentences have not reached final perfection, one should use an imperfect or improper cadence on a third, fifth, sixth, or other similar consonance. This is called avoiding the cadence, and in these avoided cadences, the voices appear to be proceeding to a perfect cadence but turn elsewhere instead (see Ex 1.2). Another method of avoiding the cadence was discussed by Loys Bourgeois (1550), who stated that cadences solmized *la sol la*, *sol fa sol*, and *re ut re* also could occur in the interrupted form *la sol*, *sol fa*, and *re ut*.[11] In this way, one of the two voice-parts creating the cadence drops out before the ultimate sonority is heard.

Ex 1.1 Perfect cadences

Ex 1.2 Avoided cadences

Zarlino (1558) informs us that all *cadenze* formed on a unison or on an octave must be approached from the closest imperfect interval and therefore must incorporate either the subsemitone or the suprasemitone.[12] Furthermore, he contends that for cadence-notes where the subsemitone does not occur naturally, for example the note G, a sharp sign does not need to be notated 'Imperoche in quella parte, che tra la penultima figura, & la ultima si trova il movimento, che ascende, sempre si intende essere collocato il Semituono ... Ma la Natura hà provisto in simil cosa: percioche non solamente li periti della Musica: ma anco li contadini, che cantano senza alcuna arte, procedeno per l'intervallo del Semituono' / 'Because in that part in which ascending motion is found between the penultimate and the ultimate notes, the semitone is always understood to be placed ... But nature has provided for this, because not only skilled musicians but also peasants, who sing without any art, proceed by the interval of the semitone' (Zarlino *IH* III 53, p 222). A number of theorists prior to Zarlino – Gaffurius (1496), Aaron (1516), Ornithoparchus (1517), Lanfranco (1533), Vanneo (1533), and Bermudo (1555) – confirm that the knowledge of this precept was widespread.[13] Bermudo's remarks on the subject are representative of the manner in which the precept was discussed: 'Imperfecta: concordantias semper sequatur proximior perfecta: puta imperfectam tertiam unisonus, perfectam quinta, imperfectam sextam quinta, perfectam octava' / 'Imperfect consonances always are followed closely by perfection: a unison follows an imperfect third, a fifth follows a perfect third, a fifth follows the imperfect sixth, and the octave follows the perfect sixth' (Bermudo *Dec* IV 48, f 87v).[14] Bermudo then goes on to amplify his comments: 'Todo lo sobredicho se guarde, no tan solamente en las clausulas: pero todas las vezes que vinieren alas consonancias perfectas de qual quier manera que sea' / 'Everything said above applies not only to *clausulae* but also to all the places in which perfect consonances are approached in any manner whatever' (Bermudo *Dec* IV 48, f 88v). Indeed, as late as 1619, the use of the subsemitone at *clausulae* where it was not marked was still being advocated: 'Es wisse doch ein jeder Cantor unnd Musicus ... bey der Clausula formali das Semitonium singen und gebrauchen musse' / 'It is known that each *Cantor* and *Musicus* ... must sing and use the *Semitonium* in the *Clausula formali*' (see Ex 1.3) (Praetorius *SM* III 3, p 31). Moreover, Loys Bourgeois (1550) specifically mentions that interrupted cadences should be performed with a subsemitone.[15]

Obviously, approaching cadence-notes from the closest imperfect interval was the norm in the sixteenth century, so much so that in 1565 the Spanish theorist Tomás de Sancta Maria established terminology

Ex 1.3 Semitone in *clausulae formales*

Table 1.1
Remisso and *sostenido* cadences

Mode	Signature	Cláusula final		Cláusula media		Cláusula passa	
1	♮	*Dsolre*	S	*Alamire*	S	—	
2	♭	*Dsolre*	S	*Ffaut*	S	*Alamire*	R
3	♮	*Elami*	R	*Csolfaut*	S	*Gsolreut*	S
4	♮	*Elami*	R	*Alamire*	S	—	
5	♭	*Ffaut*	S	*Csolfaut*	S	—	
6	♭	*Ffaut*	S	*Alamire*	R	*Csolfaut*	S
7	♮	*Gsolreut*	S	*Dlasolre*	S	—	
8	♮	*Gsolreut*	S	*Csolfaut*	S	—	

SOURCE: Sancta Maria *ATF* I 24, ff 67v–70r
Note: S = *sostenida*; R = *remissa*

to describe the two methods of creating the penultimate sonority.
Sancta Maria divided cadences into two types – those that were *remisso*
and those that were *sostenido*. The *remisso* or 'relaxed' cadence employed
a subtone in one voice and a suprasemitone in the other, whereas the
sostenido or 'sharped' cadence employed a subsemitone and a supratone.[16]
In the *sostenido* form, the subsemitonal motion to the cadence-note
frequently is not present in the voice-parts and must be added by means
of a sharp. In the *remisso* form, however, the cadence-note already is
approached from the closest imperfect interval through the semitonal
motion in the descending voice. For each of the eight modes, Sancta
Maria categorized the cadence-notes as *cláusula final*, *cláusula media*, or
cláusula passa and designated them either *remissa* or *sostenida*. A synopsis
of his classification appears in Table 1.1.

But the addition of the subsemitone was not as simple a matter as the
theorists quoted above seem to imply. Certain melodic and vertical
factors clouded the issue and demanded a degree of planning on the part
of the performer. Aaron, in his *Aggiunta* (1529), discussed a situation in
which the removal of a melodic tritone required a careful analysis of the
musical context (see Ex 1.4). In this example, a *clausula* is formed on the
final G; he therefore recommends employing a sharp on the penultimate
note rather than a flat on the dotted semibreve: 'Perche essendo da la
ragione del contrapunto ordinato che quella semibreve ultima sia p[er]
causa di una sesta che nel tenore apparira, come richiedono le naturali
cadenze sospesa, & accidentalmente pronuntiata: non è bisogno che la

Ex 1.4 Complications owing to melodic/vertical considerations

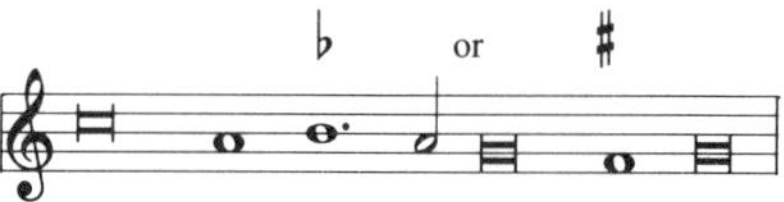

Ex 1.5 Subsemitone at *clausula* precluding its use

seconda semibreve sia dal bmolle soccorsa, ne aiutata' / 'Since the rules
of ordinary counterpoint require that the last semibreve, because of the
sixth with the tenor, be raised as in the natural cadences, and be
pronounced accidentally, it is not necessary that the second semibreve
be helped by the *b molle*' (Aaron *ToscA* f Niir).[17]

Frequently, the incorporation of the subsemitone at a *clausula* is
precluded by an upper or lower voice. In cases such as those shown in
Example 1.5, the performer had to decide which consideration should
take precedence – the need to avoid the vertical dissonance or the desire
to approach the cadence-note by the subsemitone. Tinctoris (1477),
from whom the example is taken, recognized the basic incorrectness of
the dissonance created by the subsemitone but conceded that its
incorporation was common practice: 'Concordantiae vero perfectae
quae per semitonium chromaticum, hoc est per sustentionem aut
imperfectae aut superfluae efficientur etiam sunt evitandae, licet et his
uti supra totam aut dimidiam aut maiorem partem notae mensuram
dirigentis, et perfectionem immediate praecedentis omnes fere
compositores in compositione trium aut plurium partium' / 'Indeed,
perfect consonances which through the chromatic semitone, that is, by
means of [its] support, will be imperfected [diminished] or augmented
are to be avoided. And yet virtually all composers allow these to be used
in compositions of three or more parts above all or half or the greater

Ex 1.6 Frye 'So ys emprentid' 2–3, 6–7

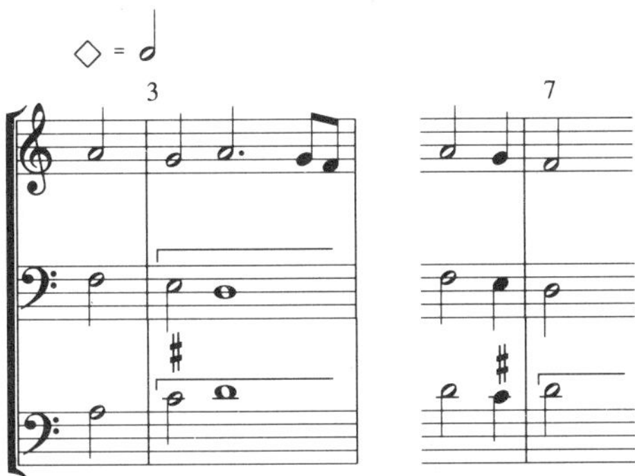

part of the note that is guiding the measure, and immediately preceding
a perfection' (Tinctoris *AC* II 34, p 144). Ramis de Pereia (1482) discussed a similar dissonance in relation to consecutive fifths: 'Tristanus
vero de silva in quinta ut ait non prohibetur totaliter quoniam potest
fieri quinta post quintam: dum tamen una sit semidiapente alia vero
diapente sicut reperimus in cantilena sois enprantis' / 'With regard to
fifths, Tristanus de Silva has said that he does not completely prohibit
[them] because a fifth is able to be placed after a fifth: as long as one is
a *semidiapente* and the other a true *diapente*, just as we find in the song
sois enprantis [Walter Frye 'So ys emprentid'; see Ex 1.6]' (Ramis *MP* pt
2, I 1). In Frye's ballade, only two pairs of consecutive fifths exist, and
in each case the sixth (E–C) expands to an octave. Presumably, Ramis
expected the Cs to be sung as C♯s, even though this produced dissonance, these were not cadential passages, and the sign *b durum* was not
indicated.[18] Thus, Ramis' example supports Bermudo's claim made
some seventy-three years later that *all* perfect consonances should be
approached from the closest imperfect interval.

However, Bermudo (1555) also suggested two ways in which the
vertical dissonance discussed by Tinctoris and Ramis could be avoided.
A simple solution to those passages where the upper voice of a minor
sixth could not be performed as *mi* was to perform the lower voice as
fa, thus producing a suprasemitonal, rather than a subsemitonal,
approach to the octave:

Quando hizieremos octava, ahora sea en clausula o de huyda,
viniendo de sexta: sera hecha con sexta mayor la qual es dicha

> perfecta, y es mas cercana de la octava, que la sexta menor. Viniendo mayor elo puntado no ay que remediars[e] pero si fuere menor remediar se ha en la boz superior con tecla negra, que es mi. Y si desta manera no se pudiere remediar por causa particular: remediar se ha en la boz baxa con una tecla negra, que es fa / Whenever we produce an octave, whether it is in a *clausula* or in passing, approaching it from a sixth, it will be done from the major sixth, which is called perfect and is closer to the octave than the minor sixth. If a major [sixth] occurs in the music, then no remedy is necessary, but if it is minor it is to be remedied in the upper voice with the black key that is *mi*. And if it cannot be remedied in this manner for a particular reason, it is to be remedied in the lower voice with the black key that is *fa*. (Bermudo *Dec* IV 48, f 88r)

Nevertheless, at another point in his treatise, Bermudo employs this vertical/horizontal quandary to introduce chromatic progressions at cadence points.[19] He acknowledges that while octaves should be approached by major sixths, some impediment, namely, vertical dissonance, may prevent the inclusion of the subsemitone. It is this desire to avoid dissonance, coupled with the need for a subsemitone at the cadence, which produced the chromatic lines in Example 1.7 (see those

Ex 1.7 Chromatic progressions at *clausulae*

sections marked with an asterisk). In each case, the subsemitone normally would have been incorporated on the first note of the bar, except that if it had been employed, dissonance would have been incurred. Therefore, the subsemitone could be applied to only the second note. Conversely, other theorists, such as Pietro Aaron (1545), prohibited this type of contrapuntal writing, because although one needs the subsemitone for the cadence, chromatic progression is forbidden.[20] Yet Hermann Finck (1556) discussed a method for solmizing these progressions, implying that chromatic passages were sung as well as played: 'Sumes igitur cis, quod Musici instrumentales sic signant C$^\ell$ quae clavis medium sonum inter C & D reddit, ita habebis ex C in C$^\ell$, mi in fa, & ex C$^\ell$ in D, iterum mi in fa' / 'If, then, one takes *Cis*, which instrumentalists mark in this way C$^\ell$, which is the sound of the *clavis* midway between C and D, then one will have *mi* to *fa* from C to C$^\ell$ and again *mi* to *fa* from C$^\ell$ to D' (Finck *PM* f Biiv). The singer's employment of chromatic passages is confirmed by Bermudo (1555), who states that even the progression C–C♯–D is sung by some.[21]

A few authors refer to a practice which, at least according to their statements, appears to have been universal.[22] Three theorists, Aaron (1529), Bermudo (1555), and Sancta Maria (1565), advocate raising the third when it occurs above a cadence-note (see Ex 1.8). Aaron maintains that this practice was so common that the necessary sign did not need to be notated: 'Ben che tal segno appresso gli dotti & pratichi cantori manco è di bisogno: ma sol si pone perche forse il mal pratico & non intelligente cantore, non darebbe pronuntia perfetta a tal positione over syllaba' / Although this sign [the sharp for raised thirds], then, is less needed by the learned and experienced singers, the *sol* [that is, the sign on the *sol*] is given because perhaps an inexperienced and unintelligent singer could not give a perfect delivery of this position or

Ex 1.8 Raised third at *clausula*

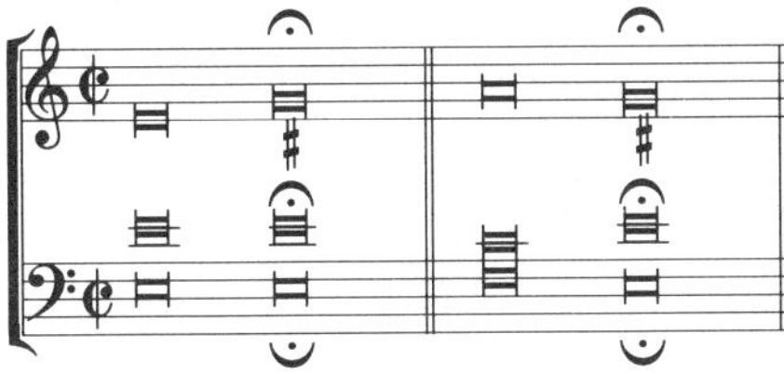

syllable [without it]' (Aaron *Tosc* II 20, f Kv). He incorporated the raised third shown in Example 1.8 because the minor tenth above the bass sounds unpleasant. The addition of the sharp, then, helped to make a sweeter sound.[23] Bermudo, citing Ornithoparchus as his authority, concurred: 'Pues digamos con Andrea, que como podemos començar en consonancia imperfecta: podemos acabar en ella. Mayormente siendo tercera mayor: la qual tiene gran perfection por el uso, que apenas ay clausula de a quatro bozes que la una no quede en dezena mayor' / 'For let us say with Andreas [Ornithoparchus] that if we can begin on imperfect consonances, we can end on them. Principally, this involves the major third, which has [such] great perfection for this use that there is scarcely a *clausula* for four voices in which one [voice] does not remain on a major tenth' (Bermudo *Dec* V 20, f 131r). Sancta Maria stated: 'Las obras comunmente fenescen en octava o en quinzena, las quales consonancias siempre an de ser sostenidas. Para lo qual es necessario que las vozes intermedias que son tenor y contraalto o la una dellas, sean puntos sostenidos. Los quales hazen que las consonancias suenen rezias y sostenidas' / 'Compositions usually end on an octave or a fifteenth, the harmony of which must always be sharped. For this reason, it is necessary that one or the other of the middle voices, that is, *tenor* or *contraltus*, be a sharped note, which makes the harmony sound strong and sharped' (Sancta Maria *ATF* I 26, f 89v).

In addition to the practices discussed above, the unnotated subsemitone was also commonly supplied in noncadential passages. Gaffurius (1496), in a chapter entitled 'De Fictae musicae contrapuncto,' mentions one such case: 'Persaepe etiam plerique pronuntiant sol sub la semitonii intervallo: quum potissime proceditur his notulis la sol la incipiendo in Alamire ... Atque item inrer [=inter] sol & fa incipiendo & terminando in Gsolreut hoc transitu sol fa sol' / 'Very often many actually pronounce *sol* below *la* as a semitonal interval, especially in the progression *la sol la* beginning on *Alamire* ... Indeed, the same occurs between *sol* and *fa* in the progression *sol fa sol*, beginning and ending in *Gsolreut*' (Gaffurius *PM* III 13, f eeiiir). Moreover, Sancta Maria's (1565) comments on the subject confirm that this procedure indeed could apply to melodic progressions quite apart from *clausulae*: 'Assi mesmo quando alguna boz hiziere, re ut re, o sol fa sol, o la sol la, por la mayor parte el ut, y el fa, y el sol, son puntos

sostenidos assi en lo natural, como en lo accidental, La razon y causa
desto es por la gracia de la solfa, y tambien porque parecen Clausulas,
las quales siempre son sostenidas, excepto haziendo mi, re, mi, que es
Clausula remissa' / 'Similarly, when any voice forms *re ut re, sol fa sol*,
or *la sol la*, the *ut, fa*, and *sol* are, for the most part, sharped both in the
natural and in the accidental [modes]. The explanation and reason for
this is the grace of the *solfa* and also because they look like *clausulae*,
the sound of which is always sharped, except when *mi re mi* is formed,
which is a *clausula remissa*' (Sancta Maria ATF I 25, f 74v). In other
words, melodic progressions solmized *re ut re, sol fa sol*, and *la sol la*
carry a semitone whether or not they actually form part of a *clausula*,
because these progressions look and presumably sound like cadences.

Similar remarks were made by Ramis de Pereia (1482),[24] and all of
the theorists quoted here on this matter underline the freedom with
which Renaissance musicians interpreted the notated page. In fact,
Ramis de Pereia expanded his discussion of the *semitonium subintel-
lectum* to include the following three melodic figures:

> Unde dicit ipse quod si cantus psallet acd et non revertatur ad
> c: quamvis deberet dici re fa sol ut ordo demonstrat. Debet
> tamen dici ut mi fa propter hoc quia ac non est semiditoni. Sed
> ditoni itercapedo aut illis met vocibus. Scilicet re fa si
> pronuntietur dicatur ditonus subintellectus / '[Johannes de
> Villanova] himself has said that if the song is sung 'acd' and
> does not return to 'c,' although *re fa sol* ought to be said (as
> regular order clearly shows), one nevertheless should say *ut mi
> fa* because of this: since 'ac' is not a semiditone but a ditone, or
> at least if *re fa* is pronounced on the same sounds, one will say
> an understood *ditonus* [that is, even though one says *re fa*, one
> actually will sing the interval *ut mi*].

> Idem quoque si cantus hunc progressum fecerit dbcdcdd et in
> suis octavis bc est tonus et cd semitonium bis factum et sic aut
> subintellecte voces tonales tenebunt semitonium aut mutatio
> fiet mi in re: que vox est coniunctarum / In the same way, if the
> song forms the progression 'dbcdcdd,' and in its octave, 'bc' is
> a *tonus* and 'cd' is twice made a *semitonium*, and so either the

hexachordal syllables carry the semitone mentally or a mutation of *mi* into *re* is made, and this note is a *coniuncta*.

Et dicit ipse ioannes es ditono semiditonum fieri hoc modo si
cantus dicut la fa sol sol non veniens iterum ad fa aut subin-
tellecte semiditonus erit aut mutatio fiat la in sol ut dicatur
la/sol mi fa fa / Johannes himself also says that a *semiditonus* is
made from a *ditonus* in this way: if the song says *la fa sol sol*
and does not come again to *fa*, either the *semiditonus* [minor
third] will be made mentally or a mutation of *la* into *sol* will be
made so that *la/sol mi fa fa* will be said. (Ramis MP pt 1, II 7)

Treatment of Vertical Dissonance

The most common dictum associated with vertical dissonance concerns the prohibition of sounding *mi* against *fa*. This precept normally
is stated as a warning to singers who might mistakenly solmize a *mi* in
one part and a *fa* in another, thus producing one of the forbidden
intervals (see Ex 1.9). Numerous theorists, however, after explicitly
prohibiting the use of *mi contra fa*, immediately qualify their position by
discussing the frequent exceptions to the rule. Zarlino's (1558) comments typify the situation: 'si dovesse mai porre la voce del Mi contra
quella del Fa, nelle consonanze perfette; come più oltra vederemo. Si
debbe però avertire, che alle volte si pone la Semidiapente ne i
Contrapunti in luogo della Diapente; similmente il Tritono in luogo
della Diatesseron, che fanno buoni effetti' / 'One must never place the
syllable *mi* against *fa* in perfect consonances, as we shall see later.
However, one should point out that at times one uses the *semidiapente*

Ex 1.9 Forbidden intervals

Ex 1.10 Permissible vertical dissonance

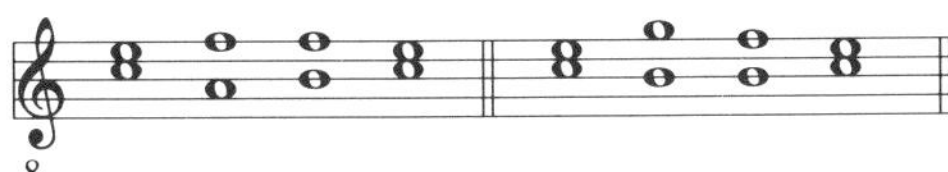

in counterpoint in place of the *diapente*, similarly the *tritono* in place of
the *diatesseron*, [both of] which make good effects' (Zarlino *IH* III 24, p
169). In a later chapter of the same treatise, Zarlino provides examples
of permissible vertical dissonance (see Ex 1.10), but he advises that the
semidiapente and *tritono* be preceded by a perfect or imperfect consonance.[25]

More than eighty years earlier, Tinctoris (1477) had discussed the
mi contra fa precept in similar terms:

> Quippe et falsum unisonum et falsum diapente et falsum
> diapason et quamlibet aliam falsum concordantiam per defec-
> tum aut superabundantiam semitonii maioris effectam evitare
> debemus. Id enim est quod in primis a magistris scholaribus
> praecipitur, ne mi contra fa in concordantiis perfectis admit-
> tant. Verumtamen saepissime apud infinitos compositores
> etiam celeberrimos oppositum comperi, ut apud Faugues ...
> apud Busnois ... et apud Caron / Indeed, we ought to avoid
> the false unison, the false fifth, the false octave, and any
> other false concord caused by the subtraction or addition of
> the major semitone. It is surely the case that masters teach
> students from the beginning that *mi* against *fa* is not permit-
> ted in perfect concords. Nevertheless, most frequently, I have
> found the opposite with innumerable composers, even the
> most famous, as with Fauges ... with Busnois ... and with
> Caron. (See Ex 1.11). (Tinctoris *AC* II 33, p 143)

Ornithoparchus (1517), on the other hand, stated the precept somewhat differently: 'In concordantiis perfectus, nuncquam ponatur vox

Ex 1.11 Permissible vertical dissonance

Ex 1.12   Proper setting of voices

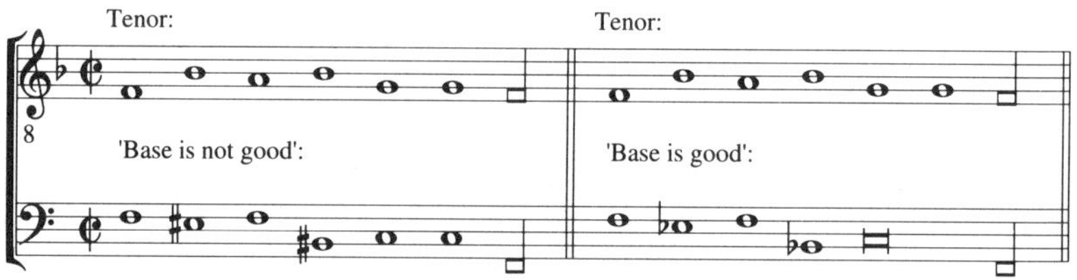

mollis contra duram: nec e contra. Sed aut mollis contra mollem, dura contra duram, aut saltem naturalem' / 'In perfect Concordances never set a sharpe Voyce against a flat, nor contrarily, but set a *Sharpe* against a *Sharpe*; a *Flat* against a *Flat*, or at least against a naturall' (see Ex 1.12) (Ornithoparchus/Dowland MAM IV 4, pp 96, 200–1). However, at least one theorist, Juan Bermudo (1555), explained why this degree of latitude was required in the correction of vertical dissonance: 'Y como los cantores tengan hecho el oydo, oyendo lo en una boz: lo usan en composicion, si primero se prepara' / 'And as a result of the way singers have trained their ears, [that is,] to hear what [is] in one voice, it [and here Bermudo is referring to the diminished fourth C♯–F] is used in composition, if it is prepared first' (Bermudo *Dec* v 32, f 139r). Bermudo then goes on to discuss the acceptable uses of the diminished fourth and other vertical dissonances. He first mentions cases in which the diminished fourth is prepared and enters on a rhythmically un-stressed part of the *compás* (see Ex 1.13).[26] Somewhat later he notes that the tritone may be used in passing, especially if it proceeds to an octave (see Ex 1.14). Following this, Bermudo treats the employment of *mi contra fa* in fifths. He states that this forbidden interval, the diminished fifth, commonly is used in cadences involving a suspension figure (see Ex 1.15) and in 'robbed' cadences (*cláusula hurtada*) (see Ex 1.16). Bermudo defines the 'robbed' cadence as a *clausula* in which one of the voices containing the *mi* against the *fa* does not proceed to the

Ex 1.13   Prepared diminished fourth

Ex 1.14 Passing tritone

expected cadence-note, but another voice does so instead.[27] The diminished fifth also may be employed in cadences if it is prepared in the way shown in Example 1.17. In this example, Bermudo asserts that the *mi contra fa* has been prepared by two things – the octave between the *altus* and the *bassus*, which removes any possible 'rudeness,' and the *tenor*'s remaining on B♭. But in order to strengthen further the case for using this dissonance, Bermudo cites Cristóbal de Morales as one of its practitioners and maintains that *mi contra fa* is frequently encountered in the works of Gombert.

Other theorists comment upon additional situations in which vertical dissonance may be employed. Aaron (1529) permits passing dissonance in rapid passages: 'Et avertisci a gli canti diminuiti, che sempre la prima nota & ultima in uno discorso diminuito, vuole esser

Ex 1.15 Cadential *mi contra fa*[28]

Ex 1.16 'Robbed' cadence

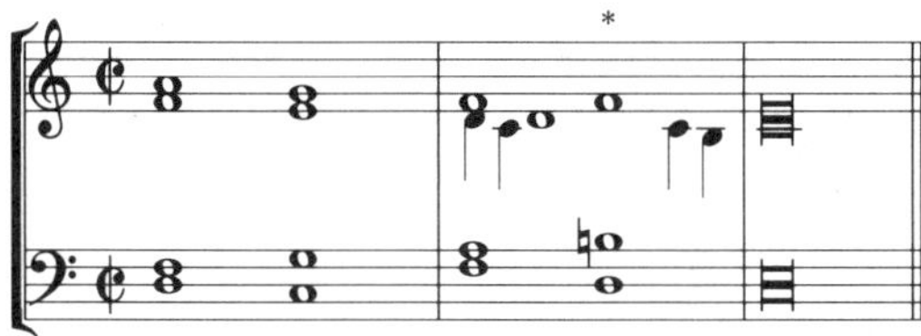

Ex 1.17 Cadential diminished fifth

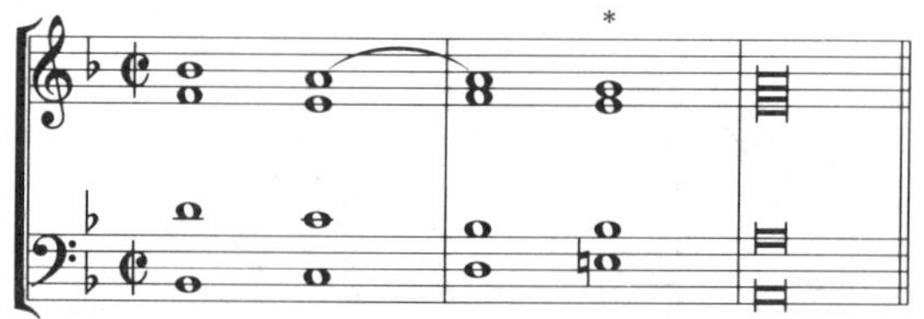

concordante: & gli mezzi diversi alquanto con dissonanze come il discorso naturale comporta: nel quale per la velocita che in se hanno le voci diminuite, essendo in essa alcune dissonanze, non sono incommode al udito del cantore' / 'And beware that in diminshed song the first and last notes in a diminished passage should always be consonant, and the middle [notes] may be diverse with as much dissonance as the passage may tolerate naturally. Because of the speed that is found in the voices with diminutions, any dissonance in the passage will not sound unpleasant to the ear of the singer' (Aaron *Tosc* II 17, f Iivr).[29] And Coclico (1552) contends that *fa* may be sung against *mi* if the note is part of a running passage.[30]

One vertical dissonance which Bermudo (1555) does not permit, however, is *mi contra fa* in an octave: 'Pero fa contra mi en octava no tiene preparacion: porque anemos de guardar la verdadera composicion del unisonus. De adonde infiero, que todas las consonancias pueden tener mas, o menos sin desabrimiento del buen oydo: pero lo octava y sus semejantes no lo suffren' / 'But *fa* against *mi* in an octave has no preparation, because we must maintain the true composition of the unisonal [consonance]. Whence it follows that all consonances can have [this dissonance] more or less without displeasure to the good ear, but the octave and similar [intervals] will not tolerate this [dissonance]' (Bermudo *Dec* V 32, f 140r). But not all theorists agreed. Francisco Correa de Arauxo (1626), citing the composers Josquin and Gombert and the theorist Francisco de Montanos (1592) as his authorities, discussed a dissonance in which an intense note sounded against a relaxed note (*punto intenso contra remisso*).[31] He observed the resultant dissonant octaves in a number of sixteenth-century compositions. In some of these works, however, Correa noted that the sign *bequadrado (b durum)*, the presence of which was necessary to create the dissonance, was omitted although reason demanded it and the force of the music

Ex 1.18 (a) Gombert 'O gloriosa Dei genitrix' 17–18
(b) Gombert 'Ay me qui vouldra' 42–3
(c) Josquin 'Pleni sunt'

required that it be there.[32] He discussed two such examples, Gombert's 'O gloriosa Dei genitrix' and 'Ay me qui vouldra,' and provided in tablature the music for another, a 'Pleni sunt' by Josquin (see Ex 1.18). In the example, the superscript signs for 'O gloriosa Dei genitrix' are derived from Correa's verbal description of the *octava mayor* which occurs at this point, and in 'Ay me qui vouldra,' the signs come from Antonio de Cabezón's (1578) intabulation of the work, to which Correa refers.[33] Correa also directs the reader's attention to a *demostración* in Francisco de Montanos' treatise, *Arte de Música* (Valladolid 1592), that contains several dissonant octaves (see Ex 1.19).

Although Correa's treatise is quite late to be included in a discussion of Renaissance matters (it was printed in 1626), his impressive documentation of the practice establishes beyond doubt that it indeed was known in the sixteenth century. Moreover, dissonant octaves certainly were known to theorists in the fifteenth century, for Tinctoris provides

Ex 1.19 *Punto intenso contra remisso* in Montanos *AM* v, ff 21v–23r

Ex 1.20 Tinctoris *AC* ii 34, bars 6–7

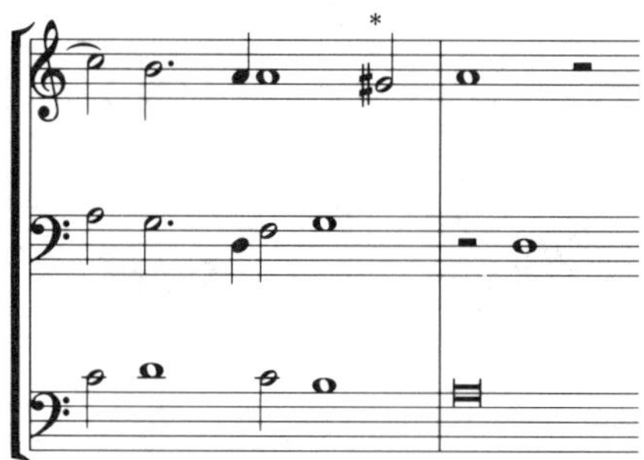

an example of one in his *Liber de arte contrapuncti* (1477) (see Ex 1.20).[34] Further evidence concerning the Renaissance use of dissonant octaves will be presented in the next chapter.

The final category of vertical dissonance that remains to be discussed is the nonharmonic or false relation. Zarlino (1558) defines these relations and prohibits them in two-part compositions:

> Onde si debbe sapere, che tanto è dire, che le parti della cantilena non habbiano tra loro relatione harmonica nelle loro voci, quanto a dire, che le parti siano vicine, o lontane l'una dall'altra per una Diapason superflua, o per una Semidiapason; overamente per una Semidiapente, o per un Tritono, o altre simili … Questi intervalli adunque, che nel modulare non si ammettono, si debbeno schivare di porti nelle cantilene di maniera, che si odino per relationi tra le parti / One should know that when it is said that the parts of a composition do not have a harmonic relation between the voices [that is, between two voices], it is the same as saying that the parts are separated from one another by a *diapason superflua* or a *semidiapason*, or by a *semidiapente* or *tritono*, or by other similar

[intervals] … These intervals, then, which are not permitted in melody should be avoided in [polyphonic] song, inasmuch as they are distasteful as regards the relations between the parts. (Zarlino *IH* III 30, p 179)

But 'nelle compositioni di più voci, parmi che tal rispetto non sia tanto necessario … cosi ancora cotali Relationi nella Musica; & alcuni altri intervalli vi sono, che da per sè danno poca dilettatione: ma accompagnati con altri fanno mirabili effetti' / 'in compositions for more voices, I believe that such respect [that is, the avoidance of nonharmonic relations] is not so necessary … yet such relations in music,

Ex 1.21 (a) Nonharmonic relations, Zarlino *IH* III 30
(b) Josquin 'Praeter rerum seriem' II 66–7[35]

along with some other intervals of similar sound, give little pleasure by themselves but make wonderful effects when accompanied by others [that is, by other types of intervals]' (Zarlino *IH* III 31, p 181). Zarlino provides an example of these nonharmonic relations (see Ex 1.21a), and one can find them in the works of many Renaissance composers (see Ex 1.21b for one such instance from Josquin).

The vertical dissonance which emerges from the nonharmonic relations discussed here almost invariably results from the voice-parts' following their own inner logic in which one voice, sounding *mi*, clashes with another, sounding *fa*. All of these types of clashes, the by-products of the vocal lines' moving somewhat independently of one another, form an integral part of compositional style in the late fifteenth and the sixteenth centuries.[36]

Treatment of Melodic Dissonance

The theorists' treatment of melodic dissonance follows a pattern similar to that of their treatment of vertical dissonance; that is, they emphatically prohibit the use of certain intervals, yet demonstrate how these forbidden intervals may be employed in composition. The following statement by Martin Agricola (1533) is typical: 'Wiewol diese iii. letzten intervalla verboten sind und ubel lauten / haben wir doch von eim glichen ein exempel gesetzt / darumb das sie unterweilen (wie wol mit unterschied der pausen) im figural ex- funden werden' / 'Although these last three intervals [*semidiapason*, *semidiapente*, and *tritonus*] are forbidden and sound bad, we nevertheless have included an example of each because now and again one will find these [intervals] in figural [music]' (Agricola *MCD* 8, f Diir). Ornithoparchus (1517), in his 'Rules for Ficta Musicke,' provides an example of how one must eschew the above-mentioned intervals when they occur as leaps in plainsong (see Ex 1.22) but, earlier in the section on chant, had illustrated the use of the tritone, describing it as a learned licence [*docta licentia*] (see Ex 1.23).[37] Furthermore, the prohibition of at least the tritone appears to have governed melodic procedure in every mode, for Tinctoris (1476) states that in chant the tritone should be

Ex 1.22 'An Exercise of Ficta Musicke'

Ex 1.23 Use of tritone

avoided in all modes, not just modes five and six.[38] A later theorist,
Nicolaus Listenius (1549), seems to have extended the prohibition
of this type of melodic dissonance to polyphony: he states that even
though he had supplied only a monophonic illustration of *cantus ficti*,
further, presumably polyphonic, examples of the practice are found
easily (see Ex 1.24).[39] Other writers confirm that this prohibition
should be applied to polyphony, and Zarlino (1558) declared that
melodic dissonance should be eliminated even if the composer had
not so indicated: 'È ben vero, che nelle modulationi si trovano alcuni
intervalli, come sono quelli di Quarta, di Quinta, & di Ottava, ne i
quali il Cantore dè porre la chorda chromatica, ancora che non sia
stata segnata dal Compositore; accioche la modulatione delle parti sia
drittamente ordinata. Ne il Compositore la debbe porre: perche è
superfluo: essendo che non si dè cantare veramente se non quelli
intervalli' / 'It is true that in [melodic] motion one finds some intervals, such as the fourth, fifth, and octave, in which the singer must
place a chromatic note (even though it had not been marked by the
composer) so that the motion of the parts will be properly disposed.
Nor must the composer mark it [the chromatic note], because it is
superfluous, for these [dissonant] intervals really should not be sung'
(Zarlino *IH* III 57, p 237). Similar remarks were made by an earlier writer,
Pietro Aaron (1529), as well: 'al quale benche non sia apparente el b
molle, appresso ogni dotto & non dotto, per ordinaria & spetial regola

Ex 1.24 *Exemplum cantus ficti*

Ex 1.25 Unavoidable tritones

da gli musichi constituita, sara inteso sempre non esser tal durezza tollerata' / 'Although *b molle* is not shown, every learned and unlearned [musician] knows as an ordinary and special rule created by musicians that this harshness never is to be tolerated' (Aaron *ToscA* f Nr).

Nevertheless, Aaron recognized that this rule would have to be broken in certain situations, and he presented three such occasions (see Ex 1.25).[40] In each case, the singer is forced to choose the lesser of two evils – to sing either the *tritono* or the *semidiapente*. He concludes that although the smaller error is to sing the *semidiapente*, the *tritono* between F and B is more acceptable in these passages (probably because it is incurred in a stepwise progression), and therefore the Bs (marked with asterisks) should not be sung as *fa*s (B♭s). However, Zarlino stated that composers could occasionally use the *semidiapente* melodically when it was suitable to the meaning of the text.[41]

Almost one hundred years later, Praetorius (1619), reproducing the same example as that given by Aaron (but with B♭ in the signature; compare Ex 1.25a with Ex 1.26), furnished two interpretations of this ambiguous passage.[42] If the melodic line rose from F to B♭ and then descended to E, the B♭ would have to be altered to B♮ (as Aaron had suggested), but if F♯ were marked, the perfect fifth between B♭ and E would be created by lowering the E.

Ex 1.26 Ambiguous melodic lines

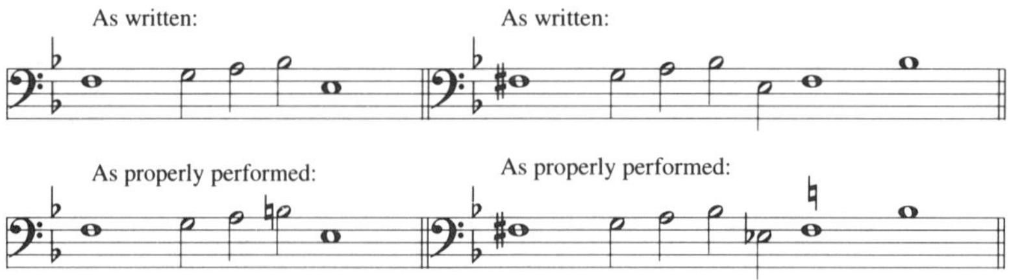

Ex 1.27 Melodic dissonance preferable to vertical dissonance

Ex 1.28 Augmented second at *clausula*

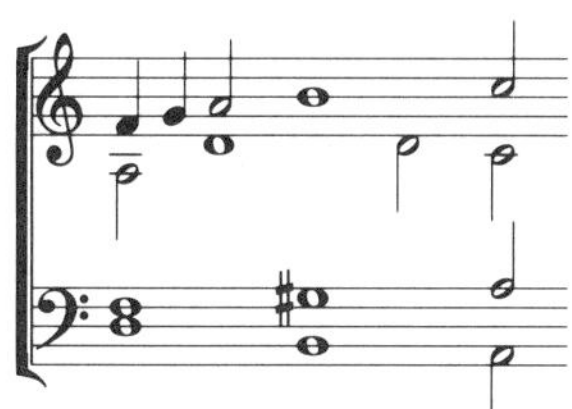

Other theorists discussed additional exceptions to the prohibition
against melodic dissonance. Tinctoris (1476), for example, remarked
that in order to avoid *mi contra fa* vertically, the composer sometimes
had to use a tritone melodically (see Ex 1.27).[43] Moreover, Bermudo
(1555) permitted the stepwise progression F–G♯ –A at a *clausula* on the
note A when another voice formed an octave with the initial F (see Ex
1.28). If, however, such a vertical impediment did not exist, then both
the F and the G would be raised.[44] He also condoned the leap of a
diminished fourth when it was prepared by a feigned cadence (*cláusula
disimulada*) (see Ex 1.29).[45] The cadence in Example 1.29 was said to be
feigned because the cadence-note D, to which the *altus* normally would
have progressed, was provided by the *tenor*, allowing the *altus* to leap to
F. Sancta Maria, on the other hand, prohibited the use of augmented
and diminished fourths and fifths in leaps; but he did permit the
augmented fifth in ascending stepwise progressions and the diminished fifth in either ascending or descending stepwise motion (see Ex

Ex 1.29 Diminished fourth at feigned cadence

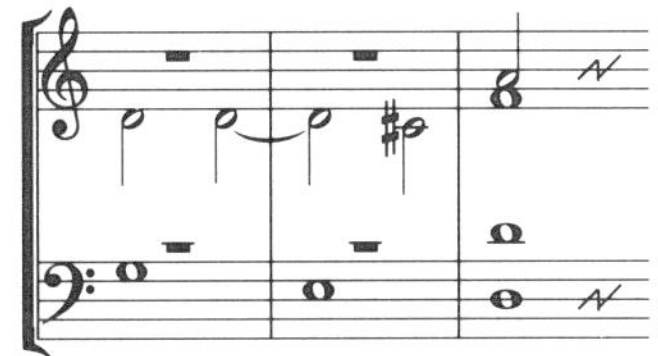

Ex 1.30 Permissible augmented and diminished fifths

1.30).[46] Similarly, Glarean (1547) disapproved of the major sixth as a leap because it was exceedingly difficult to sing.[47]

One particular convention, known throughout the sixteenth century, that some theorists discussed in relation to the tritone was eventually codified by Praetorius (1619) into the familiar phrase 'unicâ notulâ ascendente super la, semper canendum esse fa' / 'One note ascending above *la* always is sung as *fa*' (Praetorius *SM* III 3, p 31). But this convention, stated in a different form, had already been established for chant by the time of Ornithoparchus (1517): 'Quoties cantus ascendit ex Dsolre ad alamire per quintam mediate vel immediate, et ultra tantum ad secundam, cantandum est fa in bfa♮ mi in omni tono, quo ad cantus iterum dsolre tetigerit, sive signet sive non' / 'Whensoever a Song ascends from *Dsolre* to *Alamire* by a fift, mediately or immediately, and further onely to a second [ascends], you must sing *fa* in *bfa♮mi* in every *Tone* [mode], till the song do againe touch *Dsolre*, whether it be marked or no' (Ornithoparchus/Dowland *MAM* I 5, pp 21, 135). Although Ornithoparchus did not supply a musical example to demonstrate this principle, his description fits the example in Praetorius' treatise perfectly (see Ex 1.31a). The principle also applies to compositions in which the soft hexachord is employed: 'Item quando cantus non altius ascendit quam in befabemi, sive in Elami bemollari, tum semper oportet in hic canere fa' / 'Also when the song ascends no

Ex 1.31 *Fa supra la* convention

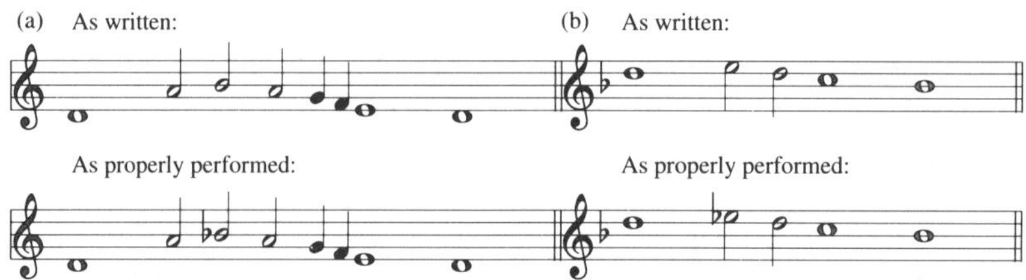

Ex 1.32 Exception to *fa supra la*

higher than *befabemi* [B] or *Elami* in *bemollari*, then one always should sing *fa* in these places' (see Ex 1.31b, which also is taken from Praetorius) (Coclico CM f Dr). Martin Agricola (1533) and Hermann Finck (1556) imply that this convention should be adopted as the normal practice in polyphony unless the sign ♮ or ♯ is written beside the note in question.[48] Moreover, Finck and Agricola represent the two ways in which this precept was discussed. Agricola, along with Ornithoparchus (1517) and Praetorius (1619), roots the practice in the prohibition of the tritone, whereas Finck, together with Coclico (1552), states the concept without reference to the tritone. Examples of the latter understanding will be presented in the next chapter.

Characteristically, however, exceptions to the precept are mentioned: 'Cassatur aut hec regula quotiens cantus ad ffaut mor non reciderit' / 'But this Rule failes, when a song doth not straightwayes fall to *Ffaut*' (Ornithoparchus/Dowland MAM I 5, pp 21, 135). By this, the author refers to a situation in which the two notes of the tritone, in this case B and F, become so widely separated that the dissonance would not be heard anyway. In addition, Aaron (1545), citing Marchettus da Padua (ca 1318), contends that in plainsong the melodic progression from D through A to B (the progression discussed by Ornithoparchus above) is frequently sung with B*mi*. This is especially true when the line proceeds past B to C, even if intervening notes occur (see Ex 1.32).[49]

Mimesis

Mimetic techniques were discussed at length by Gioseffo Zarlino (1558). He described two procedures, *fuga* and *imitatione*.[50] *Fuga* involved the literal repetition of the solmization syllables of the *guida* by the other voices, while *imitatione* referred to a structure in which this repetition was not exact. These mimetic procedures could be either *legata* or *sciolta*, that is, either strict or free. In strict writing, the entire melody is duplicated in another voice, but in free writing, the following voice proceeds independently after a certain point.

Unfortunately, Zarlino did not discuss the application of the signs *b mollis* and *b durum* to mimetic passages. However, in many of these passages, performers must determine whether the *mimesis* in question is a *fuga* or an *imitatione*; that is, they must decide whether or not the intervallic integrity of the *guida* should be maintained in the other voices. Obviously, if one wished to repeat the solmization syllables identically, then occasionally either *b mollis* or *b durum* would have to be added.

Several factors emerge from the preceding discussion which should help to further our understanding of how the addition of unnotated sharps and flats affected the level of dissonance in sixteenth-century vocal music. The incorporation of these unspecified alterations commonly arose from the desire to avoid certain types of vertical and melodic dissonance, but the theorists by no means advocated the avoidance of dissonance in all cases. In fact, some of them devoted more space to discussing the exceptions to the precepts prohibiting dissonant intervals than to presenting the precepts themselves. Nonharmonic relations were accepted by theorists, who also permitted *mi contra fa* in numerous situations involving fourths, fifths, and octaves. Even the addition of the cadential subsemitone was not necessarily precluded by the vertical constraint of the other parts. In the past, scholars have not fully recognized the importance of these factors. Nevertheless, as the intabulations of Josquin's motets will demonstrate, the exceptions played as important a role in determining normal sixteenth-century practices as did the precepts themselves.

 # TWO

Pitch-Content in Josquin's Motets

The pitch-content of Josquin's motets was interpreted in various manners during the sixteenth century. Evidence that divergent approaches were taken by Renaissance musicians was provided by the Flemish singer Ghiselin Danckerts (ca 1510–after 1565), who, in the now-famous dispute between two singers in the Roman church of S. Lorenzo in Damaso, demonstrated that more than one solution to passages containing ambiguous pitch-content was feasible.[1] Since, as this dispute aptly reveals, even the singers in one chapel could not agree on which course to follow, the contrasting interpretations encountered in the intabulations of Josquin's motets should be no surprise. The flexibility of the theoretical framework within which Renaissance musicians operated made this diversity inevitable.

But were Renaissance instrumentalists actually aware of the theoretical precepts of their own time, and if they were, did they understand how to apply these precepts in the vocal works they intabulated? That many instrumentalists understood modal theory and solmization is hardly to be doubted. Biographical information on instrumentalists active in Italy, Spain, Germany, and England confirms that a number of players regularly were employed as singers and that lutenists often played other instruments. The renowned lutenist Francesco da Milano was also a viol player and may have been the organist at the Duomo of Milan around 1530. In 1550, one Cantelmo alias Andrejolo Giov. Geronimo di Napoli, *musico*, undertook to teach a young student to play the *viola da mano*, to sing with art, and to read and write. Jean Matelart, lutenist, was appointed ca 1565 as the maestro di cappella at S. Lorenzo in Damaso, and during the 1540s the vihuelist Luis de Narvaez taught singing to the children of the chapel of Phillip II of Spain. Similarly, a number of the lutenists at the court of Mantua in the late fifteenth and early sixteenth centuries also were employed as singers.[2] The same was true in Germany in the latter half of the sixteenth century, for at least seven lutenists are known to have been singers at court or in cathedrals.[3] And in England, several of the town waits in Norwich were employed as singers in the cathedral,[4] the actor William Kemp characterizing their singing abilities as among the best in the land: 'theyr voices be admirable, everie one of them able to serve in any Cathedrall Church in Christendoome for Quiristers' (Kemp *NDW* p 17).

In addition, numerous sixteenth-century instruction books for student instrumentalists teach and stress the importance of acquiring a knowledge of modal theory, solmization, and mensural notation. The instructions on intabulating by Gerle, Bermudo, and Galilei listed in the Bibliography are cases in point. For example, Galilei states: '... non di meno io la tengho ... un'arte giuditiosissma, oltre alla quale si ricerchi non solo d'esser buon cantore, & ragioneuol contrapuntista; ma d'esser ancora ragioneuol Musico ò Theorico' / 'I hold it [the intabulation of music for instruments] to be an art calling for the greatest judgment ... in addition to which one tries not only to be a good singer, and sound contrapuntist, but also to be a sound musician, or theorist' (Galilei *FD* p 8 [trans in MacClintock *Fronimo* p 36]). Other books disclose that a knowledge of solmization was as important to the instrumentalist as it was to the singer. Sancta Maria maintained that keyboard players should understand the *solfa* (solmization) for each voice of a fantasia, singing it alone.[5] And Diego Pisador expected the vihuelist to acquire this skill as well. In his *Libro de Música* (Salamanca 1552), Pisador intabulated one of the voice-parts in each of twelve fantasias in red ciphers so that the vihuelist, with the aid of solmization syllables placed beneath each coloured cipher, could sing the part.[6] Moreover, certain books, for example those by Milán, Fuenllana, Sancta Maria, Virdung, and Judenkünig, present the tuning of the lute through solmization syllables, and this method of denoting the lute's tuning remained common until at least the 1620s.[7] Still other books, such as those by Milán, Fuenllana, and Adriansen, discuss the modes in relation to the lute. Both Milán and Fuenllana, by including the modal designation for various pieces in their collections, enable the vihuelist to observe the 'natural and accidental' cadences that may be formed in each mode.[8] Furthermore, and most important, instrumentalists strove to produce an accurate transcription and adopted the singer's linear approach when intabulating vocal music. The standard practice, as described by Adrian Le Roy in his *A briefe and plaine Instruction* (London 1574), was to cipher one part at a time, adding whatever sharps and flats were necessary.[9] As other voices were intabulated, the sharps and flats of the previously ciphered parts were adjusted to accommodate the new voice (see Ex 2.1). In the *superius* of Example 2.1, Le Roy applied the *fa supra la* convention, avoiding the melodic tritone be-

Ex 2.1 Le Roy *Inst* (1574) 'Si le bien' 65–7

tween F and B. But upon intabulating the *tenor* part, he decided that this voice needed a B♮, and he changed the *superius* from B♭ to B♮. For Le Roy, the requirements of the *tenor* obviously took precedence over the desire to avoid the tritone in the *superius*. Singers of the period could have experienced the same problem when sight-reading the chanson. The singer of the *superius* part may well have felt the need to sing B♭, the *tenor* being compelled to sing B♮. If the dissonant octave which resulted were a problem for the singers, then a solution would have to have been found. Fortunately for us today, Le Roy acted as the maître de chapelle and produced a workable solution to the problem. Once the lutenist had completed the literal transcription of the model, the final stage of the process was to add ornamentation.

In light of the evidence cited above, it is impossible to maintain that no instrumentalist was aware of solmization and other aspects of contemporary theoretical teaching. The theorist Pietro Aaron even saw fit to consult the Italian lutenist Marco Dall'Aquila (ca 1480–after 1538) on a question of music theory.[10] Thus, the evidence tends to favour the conclusion that instrumentalists and singers indeed did work within one and the same theoretical framework. The modern compartmentalization of the Renaissance use of sharps and flats into those practices employed by singers and those employed by instrumentalists is probably more imagined than real, for it is based on speculative argumentation rather than documentary evidence.[11] After all, the tablatures were produced at a time when Josquin's music was part of a living tradition, and the intabulations present versions edited by musicians who worked within that tradition. In fact, Giovanni Spataro commented upon the skill with which some instrumentalists incorporated sharps and flats: 'Dico adonca che li boni pulsatori de li instrumenti facti per arte per certa sua practica sonano li canti non come simplicemente sono composti et scripti da li indocti compositori ma li sonano come debeno esser signati: et similemente fano li periti cantori: molte volte cantano li concenti meglio che non sono stati compositi: et signati da li compositori' / 'I say, therefore, that good players of artificial instruments play songs through a certain practice not as they are simply composed and written by the unlearned composers, but play them as they should be signed. Similarly do experienced singers. Often they sing pieces better than they had been composed and signed by the composers' (Ms Vatican lat 5318, f 144v [cited and trans in Berger *Musica* p 164]).

There is no doubt in my mind that many of the sharps and flats encountered in intabulations are directly relevant to their vocal models and that the vast majority of instrumentalists examined in this book understood how to apply theoretical principles to the vocal works they intabulated. The ensuing study, then, will discuss pitch-content in the printed intabulations of Josquin's motets. Since there is no way of determining which reading(s), vocal or instrumental, Josquin might have endorsed, no study can document Josquin's own practices. What will emerge, however, is an understanding of how performers during the sixty years after his death interpreted the vocal sources of his motets.

Treatment of Cadences

The intabulations provide ample opportunity to view the cadential use of the subsemitone in five modal groups:

Dorian	'Memor esto'
Dorian *cantus mollis* (Dorian transposed to 'G' with a signature of B♭)	'Ave Maria … benedicta tu' 'Ecce, tu pulchra es' 'In exitu Israel de Aegypto' 'Pater noster' 'Praeter rerum' 'Qui habitat' 'Salve regina' 'Tribulatio et angustia'
Phrygian	'Miserere mei'
Lydian *cantus mollis* (Lydian on F with a signature of B♭)	'Absalon, fili mi' 'In principio erat verbum' 'Inviolata' 'Stabat Mater'
Mixolydian	'Benedicta es'

Table 2.1
Subsemitonal, subtonal, and suprasemitonal cadences in the motet
intabulations

Mode	Cadences (%)					
Dorian (1 motet)	Primary	D	64 sst 36 st		A	58 sst 34 st 8 sast
	Secondary	F	100 sst		E	100 sast
	Transitory	C	100 sst		G	100 st
Dorian *cantus mollis* (8 motets)	Primary	G	89 sst 11 st		D	48 sst 26 st 26 sast
	Secondary	B♭	100 sst		A	100 sast
	Transitory	F	100 sst		C	86 sst 14 st
Phrygian (1 motet)	Primary	E	100 sast		A	63 sst 37 st
	Secondary	C	100 sst		G	100 st
	Transitory	D	80 sst 20 st			
Lydian *cantus mollis* (4 motets)	Primary	F	100 sst		C	100 sst
	Secondary	A	8 sst 92 sast			
	Transitory	G	80 sst 20 st		D	90 sst 10 st
Mixolydian (1 motet)	Primary	G	100 sst		D	100 sst
	Secondary	C	100 sst			

Notes: sst = subsemitone, st = subtone, sast = suprasemitone. The
nature of the cadential part-writing was not taken into consideration in the preparation of this table.

For each of these modal groups, the occurrence of subsemitonal,
subtonal, and suprasemitonal cadences has been summarized in Table
2.1.

Clearly, many theorists overstate their case when they maintain
that all perfect intervals must be approached by the closest imperfect
interval. The norm in intabulations was, however, to do just as the
theorists recommended (to bring the penultimate interval as close as
possible to perfection), and this frequently meant adding either a sharp
or a flat. When a piece was sung in the scale of *b durum* (that is, when

no flat appeared in the signature), *clausulae* on D in Dorian and on both G and D in Mixolydian usually were approached by a subsemitone in the voice rising to the cadence-note. Cadences on A in Dorian, on the other hand, were approached either subsemitonally or suprasemitonally (that is, by adding a sharp to the rising voice or a flat to the descending voice), the nature of the part-writing determining which approach was appropriate (see below). When a piece was sung in the scale of *b mollis* in transposed Dorian (that is, when a flat appeared in the signature), *clausulae* on G were mainly rendered subsemitonally, whereas those on D were often treated either subsemitonally or suprasemitonally. In Lydian, however, cadences on F, C, G, and D were frequently subsemitonal, while A was mostly but not exclusively suprasemitonal.

The flexibility with which one could approach cadences on A in the scale of *b durum* and cadences on D and A in the scale of *b mollis* is inherent in the hexachord system itself. In *b durum*, hexachords are built on G and C (hard – GABCDE – and natural – CDEFGA), and the note B was considered to be a note of permutation. Permutation means that B could be sung as *fa* (B♭) or as *mi* (B♮), and the availability of this choice was especially important when one needed to avoid the tritone with F. B♭ is, thus, part of the system, and this presents the performer with the possibility of a B♭–A motion at cadences on A. In *b mollis*, hexachords are built on C and F (natural – CDEFGA – and soft – FGAB♭CD, with E as the note of permutation), and this makes the motion E♭–D possible.[12]

To be fair, the theoretical discussions of approaches to *clausulae* often represent simplified versions of the situations performing musicians encountered. Theorists simply could not discuss every possible ramification of their precepts. Moreover, the exceptions to the rules that they do mention, illuminating as they are, do not tell us how common these exceptional cases actually were. The intabulations, then, when coupled with the theoretical guide-lines, provide the truest reflection of contemporary practices that we can hope to obtain. A closer examination of the cadential practices encountered in the intabulations will therefore elucidate Renaissance procedures further.

Under certain conditions, the intabulators incorporated the subsemitone almost invariably. Cadences involving suspension figures (see Ex 2.2) normally carried the subsemitone regardless of whether

Ex 2.2 'Benedicta es' I 18–20 (Gintzler 1547, Teghi 1547, Phalèse 1553, Fuenllana 1554, Ochsenkun 1558, Rippe 1558, M. Newsidler 1574, and Cabezón 1578)

Ex 2.3 'Pater noster' II 30–1 (Gintzler 1547)

the cadence was primary, secondary, or transitory in function – the only exceptions being those cadences in which the suprasemitone occurred naturally and those which were rendered suprasemitonally by the intabulators.[13] This affirms Cochlaeus' and Vanneo's contention that *clausulae* solmized *re ut re* and *sol fa sol* regularly included the subsemitone.[14] However, in two of the more than two hundred cadences containing suspension figures, some of the intabulators omitted the subsemitone when it was precluded by another voice (see Ex 2.3). A small minority of the instrumentalists, notably Simon Gintzler, occasionally preferred (in contrast to Ex 2.2) to avoid incurring vertical dissonance in these cases.

A number of the intabulators omit the subsemitone at other cadence points as well. Hans Newsidler, for instance, sometimes interprets primary *clausulae*, which one would normally expect to be approached by the subsemitone, as subtonal cadences (see Ex 2.4).

Ex 2.4 'Memor esto' II 40–2, 143–5 (Newsidler 1536)

That certain primary cadences should be subtonal is understandable, however, in two-part *clausulae* where, even though one of the voices contains stock cadential ornamentation, the other voice does not proceed to the cadence-note (see Ex 2.5). Similarly, the subtonal interpretation of *clausulae* in which the subsemitone would have to be supplied by a voice not involved in the cadence is also readily comprehensible (see Ex 2.6). But the reasons for omitting the subsemitone at primary cadences where no complications arise remain elusive.[15] Nevertheless, whatever reasons a performer had for interpreting these primary cadences subtonally, his colleagues did not always agree. In 'Pater noster' (II 19), for example, Francesco da Milano, Enriquez de

Ex 2.5 'Memor esto' II 130–2 (Newsidler 1536)

Ex 2.6 'In exitu' II 31–3 (Ochsenkun 1558)

Valderrávano, and Pierre de Teghi omit the subsemitone at this
point, whereas Simon Gintzler, Sebastian Ochsenkun, and Antonio
de Cabezón prefer to specify a subsemitonal cadence (see Ex 2.7).
Analogously, Valentin Bakfark included the subsemitone in the
two-part *clausula* at bars 98–9 of 'Qui habitat,' while his German
counterparts, Hans Gerle and Sebastian Ochsenkun, chose to make
this cadence a subtonal one (see Ex 2.8).

Usually, however, the diversity discussed above was associated with
cadences in which the application of the subsemitone was precluded
by an upper or a lower voice. For example, in cases such as those shown
in Example 2.9, the incorporation of the subsemitone would produce

Ex 2.7 'Pater noster' II 18–19
(♮ Milano 1546, Valderrávano 1547,
and Teghi 1547; ♯ Gintzler 1547,
Ochsenkun 1558, and Cabezón 1578)

Ex 2.8 'Qui habitat' I 97–9 (♮ Gerle 1533
and Ochsenkun 1558; ♯ Bakfark 1565)

dissonance between the parts. And although the instrumentalists differ in their interpretation of these particular passages, the intabulations are frequently consistent in their treatment of *clausulae* with precluded subsemitones. On numerous occasions, all of the intabulators specify the subsemitone regardless of the effect on the vertical sonority (see Ex 2.10 for two such instances). But of course, even though this unanimity occurs repeatedly among the intabulations, individual instrumentalists do not always interpret this type of cadence uniformly. Sebastian Ochsenkun, for instance, incorporates the subsemitone at one primary cadence but not at another similar one (see Ex 2.11).

One circumstance does exist, however, in which the intabulators regularly excluded the subsemitone. Cadential part-writing containing doubled subtones prevented most instrumentalists from creating subsemitonal cadences (see Ex 2.12).[16] Nevertheless, if the performer

Ex 2.9 (a) 'Salve regina' 1–3 (♮ Barberiis 1546; ♯ Pisador 1552)

(b) 'Pater noster' I 30–2 (♮ Teghi 1547 and Ochsenkun 1558; ♯ Milano 1546 and Gintzler 1547)

Ex 2.10 (a) 'Inviolata' I 56–8 (Gerle 1533, Valderrávano 1547, Ochsenkun 1558, and Cabezón 1578)
(b) 'Qui habitat' I 103–5 (Gerle 1533, Ochsenkun 1558, and Bakfark 1565)

wished to include a subsemitone at one of these cadences, he could do one of two things – omit the restrictive voice or produce a *punto intenso contra remisso*. The first solution was favoured by Simon Gintzler and Albert de Rippe in 'Praeter rerum' (see Ex 2.13), and the second was

Ex 2.11 'In exitu' II 49–50; III 18–19 (Ochsenkun 1558)

Ex 2.12 'Salve regina' 23–5 (Barberiis 1546 and Pisador 1552)

Ex 2.13 'Praeter rerum' I 42–3 (Gintzler 1547 and Rippe 1555)

*omitted

Ex 2.14 (a) 'Stabat Mater' I 13–15 (Ochsenkun 1558)
(b) 'Pater noster' II 12–13 (Milano 1546)

1. This note is rendered as a
minim by Ochsenkun.

Ex 2.15 'Benedicta es' I 84–5 (Phalèse 1553)

adopted by Sebastian Ochsenkun in 'Stabat Mater' and by Francesco da Milano in 'Pater noster' (see Ex 2.14).

Thus, the inclusion of the subsemitone at cadences where its application was precluded appears to have been governed by the level of dissonance that particular musicians desired in their performances. As Tinctoris remarked, '*virtually all* composers [use this dissonance] immediately preceding a perfection in compositions of three or more parts.'[17]

On one occasion, a single intabulator, Pierre Phalèse, chose to use a subsemitonal approach to both the octave and the fifth of the cadence (see Ex 2.15). The other six intabulators followed the more normal sixteenth-century practice and employed the subsemitone only in the voice rising by step to the octave. This example from Josquin appears to support the contention that secondary subsemitones were, for the most part, unfashionable in the sixteenth century.[18]

Frequently, the intabulators' interpretations of certain types of cadential part-writing produced chromaticism within single voice-parts. This practice most commonly is encountered in passages such as

Ex 2.16 (a) 'Memor esto' I 63–4 (Newsidler 1536)
       (b) 'Salve regina' 37–8 (Pisador 1552)[19]
       (c) 'Benedicta es' I 4–5 (Phalèse 1553 and Fuenllana 1554)

that in Example 2.16. In these cadential figures, the chromaticism results from the subsemitone's being applied to only the penultimate note of the *clausula*. The instrumentalists who rendered these types of

Ex 2.17 (a) 'Pater noster' I 100–1 (Ochsenkun 1558)
(b) 'Pater noster' I 114–15 (Milano 1546)
(c) 'Benedicta es' I 102–3 (Cabezón 1578)

passages chromatically include Hans Newsidler, Miguel de Fuenllana, Diego Pisador, and Pierre Phalèse.[20] Other musicians, especially Francesco da Milano, Sebastian Ochsenkun, and Antonio de Cabezón, introduced these same chromatic lines through the ornamentation that they added at cadence points (see Ex 2.17).

A striking chromatic progression occurs in Simon Gintzler's intabulation of 'Stabat Mater' (see Ex 2.18). Gintzler, in following normal intabulation procedure, divides the *tenor*'s *longa* into shorter note values, thereby providing the opportunity for the creation of a subsemitonal cadence on D. By using ornamentation as the vehicle for incorporating the subsemitone, Gintzler is able to approach the cadence-note from the closest imperfect interval.

Further examples of chromatic progressions at cadence points are found in the intabulations by Hans Gerle. Gerle occasionally embel-

Ex 2.18 'Stabat Mater' I 65–7 (Gintzler 1547)

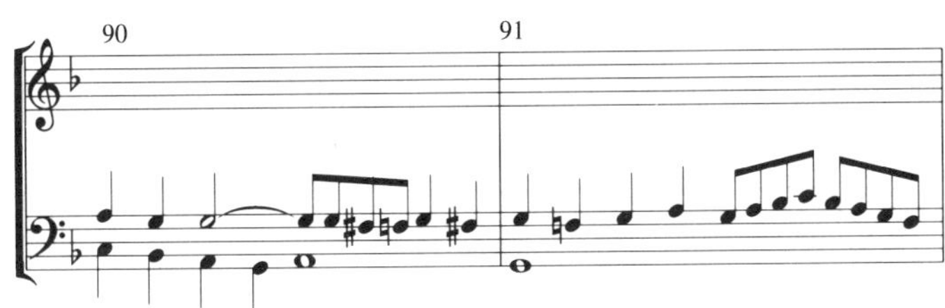

Ex 2.19 'Qui habitat' II 90–1 (Gerle 1533)

Ex 2.20 'Mille regretz' 23 (H. Newsidler 1536)

Ex 2.21 (a) 'Qui habitat' II 16–17 (Ochsenkun 1558)

(b) 'Pater noster' I 118–19 (Milano 1546)

Ex 2.22 'Pater noster' II 48–9 (Valderrávano 1547)

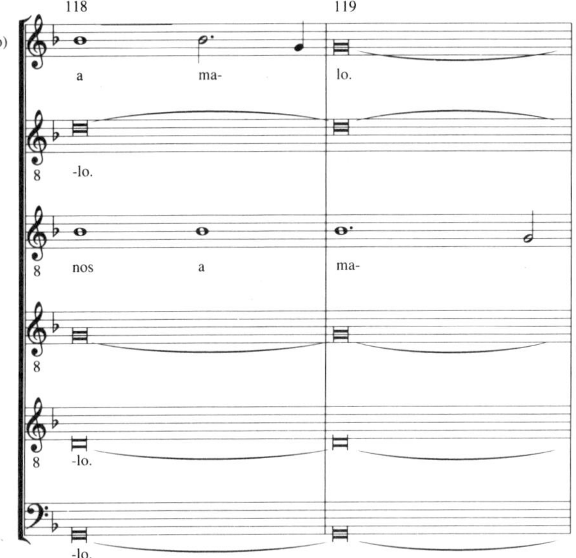

Ex 2.23 (a) 'Tribulatio et angustia' [*cantus mollis* Dorian]
20–1 (Phalèse 1552)
(b) 'Memor esto' [Dorian] I 115–17 (H. Newsidler 1536)

lishes *clausulae* with the figure shown in Example 2.19. That this
chromatic line is not a misprint for

can be established by the fact that he also uses the same chromatic
figure earlier in 'Qui habitat' (see I 78–9) and the fact that other lutenists employed similar progressions. For instance, Hans Newsidler,

Ex 2.24 'Pater noster' II 10–13 (Gintzler 1547,
Valderrávano 1547, Teghi 1547, Ochsenkun 1558, and
Cabezón 1578)

in his arrangement of Josquin's 'Mille regretz,' ornamented one
primary *clausula* with the figure in Example 2.20.

Although all of the chromatic lines referred to above involve the
part which rises by step to the cadence-note, chromaticism could also
occur in the voice which descends by step (see Ex 2.22). In the
example, Enriquez de Valderrávano aligned himself with normal
practice and opted for a suprasemitonal approach to the cadence-note
D. However, unlike the other intabulators of this motet, Valderrávano
incorporated the E♭ only on the penultimate note of the *clausula*,
creating the chromatic line D–E–D–E♭–D.

Certain intabulators even used ornamentation to introduce cadential
subsemitones in places where the required notes did not exist in the
vocal model. Both Sebastian Ochsenkun and Francesco da Milano
provide examples of this practice (see Ex 2.21).

A number of *clausulae* could be interpreted either as suprasemitonal
or as subsemitonal cadences. In cases such as those shown in Example

Ex 2.25 'Pater noster' II 42–3 (Milano 1546, Gintzler 1547, Valderrávano 1547, Teghi 1547, Ochsenkun 1558, and Cabezón 1578)

Ex 2.26 'Praeter rerum' I 46–8 (Gintzler 1547, Fuenllana 1554, Rippe 1555, and Ochsenkun 1558)

2.23, the approach to the *repercussio* from the closest imperfect interval could be achieved in one of two ways – by incorporating either a flat or a sharp.

However, when *clausulae* involved three or more voices, the nature of the part-writing frequently channelled the intabulators' thinking in a single direction. For example, cadences on the *repercussio* in *cantus mollis* Dorian invariably were treated subtonally when the part-writing contained a doubling of the two voices creating the cadence, that is, when it contained doubled Cs and Es (see Ex 2.24). But if E alone were doubled, then a subsemitonal approach was used (see Ex 2.25). Conversely, if only C were doubled, then the approach was suprasemitonal (see Ex 2.26). Moreover, when the pitch A was added to the doubled Cs, preventing a lowering of the E, a subtonal cadence resulted (see Ex 2.27); yet in a different vertical context (one without doubled Cs), the note A suggested to the intabulators that a subsemitonal *clausula* was

Ex 2.27 'Salve regina' 23–5 (Barberiis 1546 and Pisador 1552)

Ex 2.28 'Tribulatio et angustia' 47–9
(Phalèse 1552)

Ex 2.29 'Qui habitat' I 132–3
(Gerle 1533, Ochsenkun
1558, and Bakfark 1565)

more appropriate (see Ex 2.28). On the other hand, *mi contra fa* between E and B♭, led the intabulators to opt for a suprasemitonal cadence (see Ex 2.29).

Nevertheless, in one vertical context, the intabulations do exhibit a variety of approaches to *clausulae* on the *repercussio* D (see Ex 2.30a).

Ex 2.30 (a) 'Qui habitat' II 69–70 (E♭ Gerle 1533; C♯
Ochsenkun 1558 and Bakfark 1565)
(b) 'Pater noster' I 96–7 (subtonal interpretation – Gintzler
1547 and Ochsenkun 1558; E♭ Teghi 1547; C♯ Milano 1546)

When the note G is present in the sonority, two procedures appear to
be equally common. Some musicians raise the C and incur the dissonance of C♯ against G, while others lower the E, presumably to avoid
this dissonance. Quite independent of these two traditions, however,
are German lutenists, who were just as likely to treat this type of
cadence subtonally as they were to treat it either subsemitonally or
suprasemitonally (see Ex 2.30b).[21]

Even *clausulae* on A in *cantus mollis* Dorian could be rendered either
subsemitonally or suprasemitonally. Francesco da Milano approached
one such cadence in the manner shown in Example 2.31. Perhaps
Francesco used the G♯/B♮ sonority within the scale of *b mollis* to
make this important cadential point more prominent.

Many cadences in Josquin's motets are approached by a melodic

Ex 2.31 'Pater noster' I 37–9 (Milano 1546)

progression in the lowest sounding voice which might best be described as a 6–5–1 formula.[22] In these progressions, the sixth step frequently is lowered in those modes where a tritone might occur between this step and a previous note. For example, cadences on the note G in *cantus mollis* Dorian often are approached B♭ ... E–D–G, and in this progression the E is lowered by most, but not all, of the intabulators (see Ex 2.32). In fact, this flattening occurs even when the tritone is not present and the incorporation of the flat produces a nonharmonic relation between the parts (see Ex 2.33).

However, a wide variety of procedures can be found, and one should not make this practice appear to be more common than it

Ex 2.32 'Pater noster' I 50–3 (♭ Milano 1546, Teghi 1547, and Ochsenkun 1558; ♮ Gintzler 1547)

Ex 2.33 'Pater noster' I 100–1 (♭ Milano 1546, Teghi 1547, and Ochsenkun 1558; ♮ Gintzler 1547)

Ex 2.34 (a) 'Memor esto' I 64–6 (Newsidler 1536)
(b) 'Praeter rerum' II 36–8 (♮ Rippe 1555 and Ochsenkun 1558; ♭ Gintzler 1547)
(c) 'Pater noster' I 24–6 (Milano 1546, Gintzler 1547, Teghi 1547, and Ochsenkun 1558)

actually was.[23] Intabulators frequently left the sixth step unaltered even though the tritone was present (see Ex 2.32 and Ex 2.34a), and though vertical *mi contra fa* just before the 6–5–1 formula increased the desirability of a flattened sixth approach to the cadence (see Ex 2.34b). They also retained the E♮ when the sixth step was simply a passing note near the cadence (see Ex 2.34c). Moreover, according to the

Ex 2.35 'Pater noster' II 76–end

Ex 2.36 'Pater noster' I 55–9 (Milano 1546 and Gintzler 1547)

in ter- ra. Pa-
sic- ut in cae- lo et in ter- ra.
sic- ut in cae- lo et in ter- ra.
et in ter- ra.
sic- ut in cae- lo et in ter- ra.
sic- ut in cae- lo et in ter- ra

intabulations of 'Benedicta es,' the sixth step also was not lowered when the progression E–D–G occurred in the Mixolydian mode, presumably because no tritonal problems existed between B and E.

The final category of cadential procedure that remains to be discussed concerns the raising of thirds above cadence-notes. The intabulators exhibit a wide variety of practices in this regard which demonstrates that the theorists' statements on this matter were by no means universally applied.[24] The *clausula* shown in Example 2.35 typifies the diversity of approach. Only four of the six instrumentalists raise the third, and interestingly, this produces chromaticism (B♭–B♮) in the intabulations by Francesco da Milano and Simon Gintzler. The division of the *quinta vox's longa* into shorter values enabled both lutenists to delay the incorporation of the B♮ until the very last moment.

The vocal sources of the five motets, 'Benedicta es,' 'Inviolata,' 'Pater noster,' 'Praeter rerum,' and 'Stabat Mater,' for which I have collected variants never specify the raised third except for one occasion in the *secunda pars* of 'Inviolata.' At the final cadence, sharp signs are notated in the manuscript Modena, Duomo, Biblioteca e Archivio Capitolare, ms Mus IX, indicating that this cadence is to contain the raised third. Antonio de Cabezón is the sole intabulator to incorporate this raised third, as both Hans Gerle and Sebastian Ochsenkun leave the note uninflected.

Another passage in 'Pater noster' (I 55–9) shows how raised thirds were applied to *clausulae* occurring within the work (see Ex 2.36). Both of the cadences in the example (bars 55–6, 58–9) are on the *finalis* of the mode, *cantus mollis* Dorian, and in each case Josquin includes a B♭ in the sonority. Two of the four intabulators, Milano and Gintzler, alter this note to B♮, following the recommendations of those theorists who advocate raising the third at cadences. Evidently, this was normal Renaissance procedure even when, as this example demonstrates, the voice containing the third begins a new phrase at the cadence point.[25]

Noncadential Uses of the Semitone

The intabulations tend to confirm statements made by theorists that progressions solmized *la sol la*, *sol fa sol*, and *re ut re* could be sung with a semitone.[26] Josquin's motets offer numerous opportunities for us to verify this assertion, and Example 2.37 presents a selection of the passages concerned. In this example, the inclusion of the semitone creates melodic nonharmonic relations with the previous and following unaltered notes. Although these false relations did not preclude the incorporation of the semitone, the prohibition against *mi contra fa* did force Francesco da Milano to omit the semitone in at least the passage shown in Example 2.38 (compare the *bassus* and *superius* ornamental figures). However, even when vertical constraints were not present, this semitone principle never was applied each time the opportunity to do so arose. Miguel de Fuenllana, for instance, treats certain figures differently on each repetition (see Ex 2.39).

A number of intabulators introduce the subsemitone in passages which do not lead to a cadence. The strong pull to the structural

Ex 2.37 (a) 'Pater noster' II 46–7 (Milano 1546 and Valderrávano 1547)
(b)'Salve regina' 62–3, 69–70 (Pisador 1552)
(c) 'In principio' 27–8 (Pisador 1552)

Ex 2.38 'Stabat Mater' I 29 (Milano before 1536)

Ex 2.39 'Benedicta es' I 3–4, 7–8 (Fuenllana 1554)

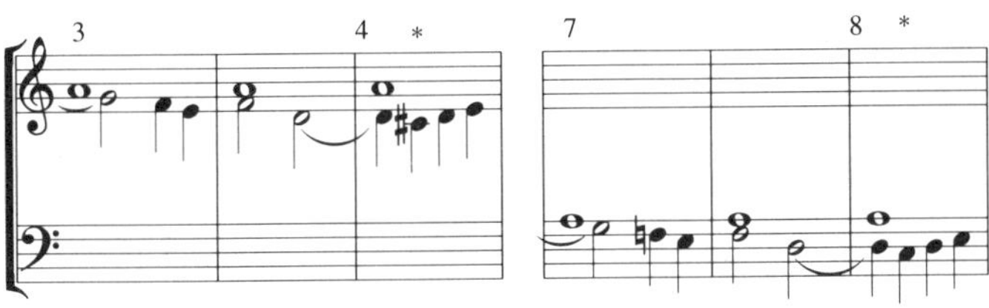

foundations of the modes, that is, the *finalis* and the *repercussio*, frequently led the instrumentalists to approach perfect intervals from the closest imperfect interval even if the notes involved were not part of a *clausula*. Thus, the intabulations support Bermudo's claim that this practice applies beyond cadential situations.[27] The passages shown in Example 2.40 are typical.

Treatment of Vertical Dissonance

The intabulations provide numerous examples of passages in which *mi contra fa* was both eliminated and retained. The most common method of removing this dissonance was through the introduction of a flat, and on several occasions virtually all of the sources, both vocal and instrumental, were in complete agreement.[28] In the *prima pars* of 'Pater noster,' for instance, *mi contra fa* was eliminated in every source, except one vocal manuscript, in each of the cases shown in Example 2.41. Today, one might consider the simultaneous sounding of E against B♭ in these examples to be an obvious application of the theorists' dictum

Ex 2.40 (a) Mixolydian: 'Benedicta es' I 39–40 (Gintzler 1547, Ochsenkun 1558, Rippe 1558, M. Newsidler 1574, and Cabezón 1578)[29]

(b) Lydian *cantus mollis*: 'Inviolata' III 25–6 (Valderrávano 1547)

(c) Dorian *cantus mollis*: 'Qui habitat' I 49–50 (Bakfark 1565)

prohibiting *mi contra fa*, but such an approach, the most common in the intabulations, was not taken in other similar situations. In at least eighteen separate passages, *mi* against *fa* was retained in the intabulations. Example 2.42 presents four instances of this practice.

Ex 2.41 'Pater noster' I 41, 45, 92 (Milano 1546, Gintzler
1547, Teghi 1547, and Ochsenkun 1558)

Throughout these four examples, no consensus exists among the
intabulators, and both the removal and the retention of the dissonance
appear to have been within the sphere of normal practice. Bermudo
(1555), in fact, probably would have condoned the *mi contra fa* in parts
(a) and (b), because in 'Qui habitat,' the dissonance is prepared by the
repeated B♭, and in 'Stabat Mater,' the E proceeds directly to an octave
on F. The momentary passing dissonance in 'In exitu' was obviously
inoffensive to one intabulator, the German lutenist Sebastian
Ochsenkun, but the treatment of the vertical tritone between F and B
in 'Benedicta es' was complicated by melodic considerations. This last
passage, which embodies the classic dilemma cited by Pietro Aaron
(1529),[30] contains both linear and vertical F–B tritones, and the
performer must decide which consideration, melodic or harmonic,
should take precedence. Three of the intabulators (Teghi, Fuenllana,

Ex 2.42 (a) 'Qui habitat' I 8–10 (Ochsenkun 1558 and Bakfark 1565)

(b) 'Stabat Mater' I 50–2 (Ochsenkun 1558 and Cabezón 1578)

(c) 'In exitu' I 134–5 (Ochsenkun 1558)

(d) 'Benedicta es' I 83–5 (♮♯Teghi 1547, Fuenllana 1554, and Ochsenkun 1558; ♭♯Phalèse 1553 and Cabezón 1578; ♮♯Gintzler 1547, Rippe 1558, and M. Newsidler 1574)

Ex 2.43 (a) 'In exitu' II 57–9 (Ochsenkun 1558)
(b) 'Memor esto' I 44–6 (H. Newsidler 1536)

and Ochsenkun) give priority to the melodic consideration and eliminate only the *tenor*'s linear tritone by raising the F in bar 84. The
remaining five intabulators, however, regard both factors to be of equal
importance. Each of the performers in this latter group removes the
melodic tritone by raising the *tenor*'s F in bar 84 for the cadence, but
eliminates the vertical tritone in either of two ways: some (Phalèse and
Cabezón) lower the *tenor*'s B♮ (bar 83) through the *fa supra la* con-

Ex 2.44 (a) 'Praeter rerum' I 61–2 (Fuenllana 1554)
         (b) 'In exitu' I 67–8 (Ochsenkun 1558)

Ex 2.45 'Qui habitat' I 97–9 (Ochsenkun 1558)

vention, while others (Gintzler, Rippe, and M. Newsidler) raise the
bassus' F (bar 83) in preparation for the cadence. The mode of this work,
Mixolydian, does not seem to have influenced the choice of Phalèse

and Cabezón. One might argue, as Karol Berger has done, that flats were avoided altogether or were used very rarely in this mode because they transformed Mixolydian into transposed Dorian (that is, Dorian on G with a B♭ in the signature).[31] But as the example demonstrates, this view was not held by all sixteenth-century musicians, and our notion of modal purity probably should be adjusted to reflect the flexible practices of the period. All of these solutions were independently adopted by more than one performer and represent standard Renaissance procedure.[32] Thus, depending on the context in which the dissonance occurs, sharps or flats could be used to remove *mi contra fa*.

The intabulations substantiate Zarlino's claim that in compositions for many voices it was not so vital to avoid nonharmonic relations.[33] Moreover, the frequency with which the *mi-fa* clash occurs in the intabulations suggests that these clashes were an important part of the Renaissance 'sound ideal.' Repeatedly, these false relations reveal that the sixteenth-century musician must have regarded this type of dissonance as a normal part of the style. In each of Examples 2.43 to 2.45, the dissonance occurs as a by-product of the linear thinking which both singers and instrumentalists applied to the performance of vocal music. Thus, the voice-parts are governed by their own inner logic and generate the types of nonharmonic relations that Renaissance musicians expected to incur; in Bermudo's words, 'as a result of the way singers have trained their ears, [that is,] to hear what [is] in one voice, it [and here he is referring to the vertical diminished fourth C♯–F] is used in composition, if it is prepared first.'[34]

The nature of Josquin's part-writing is such that the *mi* and *fa* often are separated in time by a minim or by a semibreve, and the effect of the dissonant octave or unison is thereby weakened (see Ex 2.43). But when the two notes are adjacent to one another, the clash becomes most striking (see Ex 2.44). The relations exhibited in this last example are predictable by-products of the independent interactions of the voice-parts. The dissonance encountered in 'In exitu,' for instance, results from an E*fa*, introduced to avoid *mi contra fa*, between the *tenor* and the *bassus*, that clashes with the E*mi* of the *altus*. Inevitably, these relations are found even in two-part writing, where Zarlino expressly prohibits them (see Ex 2.45).[35]

Ex 2.46 'Benedicta es' I 64–5

Ex 2.47 Lupi 'Benedictus dominus' I 21–3
(Gintzler 1547)

The simultaneous sounding of dissonant octaves (*punto intenso contra remisso*) is employed by the intabulators when the part-writing warrants such a treatment. In 'Benedicta es' (see Ex 2.46), three of the musicians (Teghi, Ochsenkun, and Cabezón) chose to incur the disso-

Ex 2.48 (a) 'Inviolata' I 20–1 (Gerle 1533 and Valderrávano 1547)

(b) 'Qui habitat' I 41 (Gerle 1533)

Ex 2.49 'Qui habitat' I 89–90 (Gerle 1533)

nance F♯/F between the *superius* and the *quinta vox*. Two others (Gintzler and M. Newsidler) inflected both the Fs, while Fuenllana and Rippe omitted the *quinta vox* at this point.

A similar dissonance is employed by Simon Gintzler in Johannes Lupi's motet 'Benedictus dominus.'[36] In the cadential passage shown in Example 2.47, Gintzler lowered the Bs in the *superius* and *bassus* in order to remove melodic tritones. But since he also wished to create a secondary subsemitone to the *tenor*'s C, he incorporated B♮, and this caused the dissonant *mi-fa* clash. Thus, each voice followed its own inner logic – further demonstration that voice-parts could indeed proceed independently of one another.[37]

These dissonant octaves also were employed within the ornamentation that various instrumentalists added to the vocal modal. This occurred in both cadential (see Ex 2.48) and noncadential (see Ex 2.49) passages.[38]

Treatment of Melodic Dissonance

The intabulations reflect the flexibility with which the theorists discuss the prohibition of the melodic tritone. The instrumentalists regularly eliminate the tritone, whether it emerges in a stepwise progression or as a leap (see Ex 2.50). But when more than one solution to a problematic passage is feasible, the performers exhibit their individual predilections. In 'Pater noster,' for instance (see Ex 2.51), the stipulation of a flat to remove the melodic tritone in the *sexta vox* creates a nonharmonic relation with the E♮ introduced into the cadential ornamentation. Pierre de Teghi, Sebastian Ochsenkun, and Antonio de Cabezón choose to incur this false relation, a by-product of the independent working of the *sexta vox* and the *superius* with respect to each other, whereas Francesco da Milano, Simon Gintzler, and Enriquez de Valderrávano prefer the opposite, that is, to incur the melodic tritone in order to avoid the nonharmonic relation.

Furthermore, the introduction of a flat to remove the tritone could, at times, create *mi contra fa*. In the passage shown in Example 2.52, the intabulator, Sebastian Ochsenkun, obviously was more

Ex 2.50　(a) 'Qui habitat' i 105–9 (Gerle 1533, Ochsenkun
1558, and Bakfark 1565)
(b) 'Stabat Mater' i 33–4 (Milano before 1536, Gintzler
1547, Phalèse 1553, Ochsenkun 1558, and Cabezón 1578)

concerned with eliminating the linear dissonance than he was with
avoiding *mi* against *fa*.

In all of the passages just cited, the intabulators use an E♭ to remove
the tritone B♭–E, and this appears to have been the normal sixteenth-
century procedure. However, in certain contexts, the B♭ could be raised
instead, and an example of this is found in two of the intabulations of

Ex 2.51 'Pater noster' II 67–8

Ex 2.52 'In exitu' III 106–8 (Ochsenkun 1558)

'Praeter rerum.' In Example 2.53, both Rippe and Ochsenkun remove the tritone in the *tenor secundus* by lowering the E but in the *bassus secundus* by raising the B♭. Presumably, they wished to treat the melodic line C–B♭–C as one of those *sol-fa-sol* progressions which could be sung with the semitone. Other intabulators viewed this passage differently, and Simon Gintzler specified E♭s and B♭s throughout this section.

Further evidence that raised notes were used to remove tritones is found in Claude Gervaise's dance book *Second livre contenant trois Gaillardes* ... (Paris 1547). In the passage quoted in Example 2.54, F*mi*, employed as a raised third above the cadence-note, eliminates the dissonance. But an equally acceptable alternative is to employ B*fa*, and this is how the brothers Paul and Bartholomeus Hessen interpreted the passage (*Viel feiner lieblicher stücklein Spanischer, Welscher, Englischer, Französischer composition und tenz* [Breslau 1555] no 202).[39]

The intabulators frequently applied the *fa supra la* convention to Josquin's motets even when the melodic tritone itself, probably the reason for the convention, was not present. Repeatedly, the progressions A–B–A (Dorian mode) and D–E–D (transposed Dorian) were rendered with flats (see Ex 2.55). However, as with most of the other practices discussed in this book, the instrumentalists treated certain passages in various ways. In fact, the *fa supra la* convention was not

Ex 2.53 'Praeter rerum' I 58–60 (Rippe 1555 and
Ochsenkun 1558)

Ex 2.54 *Second livre* ... , 'Pavane' (F♯ Gervaise 1547;
B♭ Hessen 1555)

Ex 2.55 (a) 'Memor esto' I 112–13 (H. Newsidler 1536)
(b) 'Ave Maria' 33–5 (Spinacino 1507)

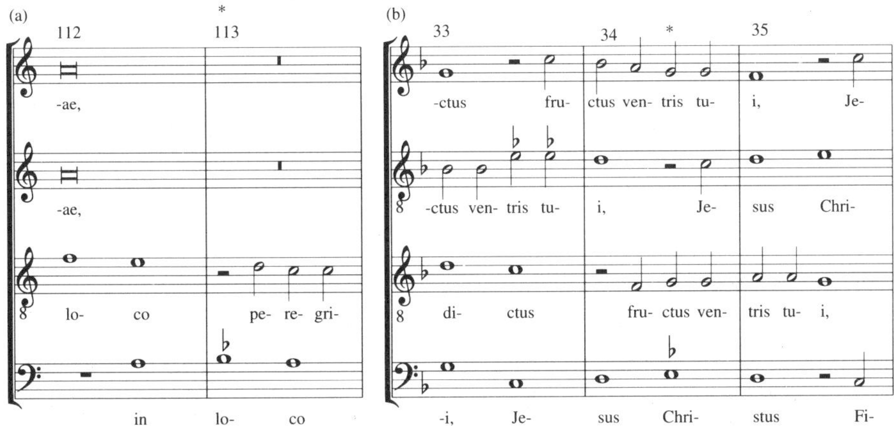

Ex 2.56 'Pater noster' II 49–51 (♮ Milano 1546,
Valderrávano 1547, Ochsenkun 1558, and Cabezón 1578;
♭ Gintzler 1547 and Teghi 1547)

applied by all the performers every time the opportunity arose, and in Example 2.56, four of the six intabulators chose to retain the E♮ in the *bassus*, presumably because the note B♭ does not occur in the phrase.

Mimesis and Repeated Material

The intabulations document the degree to which the various instrumentalists interpreted the pitch-content of mimetic passages consistently. As one would expect, no uniform practice exists. For example, some instrumentalists treated a mimetic passage in 'Qui habitat' as a *fuga*, whereas at least one other performer treated it as an *imitatione* (see Ex 2.57).

Even in canonic writing, the *comes* voice need not duplicate the intervals of the *dux* consistently, particularly at *clausulae*. In certain contexts, the desire for a subsemitonal approach to the cadence might require the performer to modify one of the voices slightly. 'Inviolata,' for instance, contains a canon at the fifth between the *tenor primus* and the *tenor secundus* in which the *dux* cadences on A and the *comes* on E (see Ex 2.58). The nature of the part-writing leading to the *clausula*

Ex 2.57 'Qui habitat' I 32–7 (*fuga* – Ochsenkun 1558 and Bakfark 1565; *imitatione* – Gerle 1533)

Ex 2.58 'Inviolata' I 52–6 (Cabezón 1578)

on A is such that if one wished to avoid the vertical dissonance between E and B♭ by raising the *superius'* B♮, then the only way of approaching the cadence-note from the closest imperfect interval is to sharpen the *dux*'s G, and this is precisely the manner in which one intabulator, Antonio de Cabezón, rendered the passage. However, this same sharpening is not required in the *comes*, because no vertical impediment obstructs the normal suprasemitonal approach to the cadence-note E.

A similar diversity of approach exists in the intabulations of 'Pater noster.' The section of the motet shown in Example 2.59 is stated four times in succession, and the instrumentalists adopted several solutions to the pitch-content of this passage. Three of them uniformly applied their solutions to each repetition, but three performers, Francesco da Milano, Sebastian Ochsenkun, and Antonio de Cabezón, vary their interpretations of this passage on its successive restatements.

All of these examples demonstrate that the consistent application of the precepts and conventions discussed in Chapter 1 was not of primary concern to all the instrumentalists. Indeed, uniform treatment of repeated material seems outside the practices of many sixteenth-century musicians.

Ex 2.59 'Pater noster' II 46–9

1 - 4	Gintzler 1547	e♭	f♮		e♭	f♮	e♭	
	Teghi 1547	e♭	f♮		e♭	f♮	e♭	
	Valderravano 1547	e♮	f♯		e♮	f♮	e♭	

Francesco 1546	1	e♮	f♯		e♭	f♮	e♮	
	2	e♮	f♮		e♮	f♮	omits	
	3	e♮	f♮		e♭	f♮	e♮	
	4	e♮	f♮		e♮	f♮	e♮	

Ochsenkun 1558	1 & 2	e♮	f♮	e♭	f♮	e♭	
	3 & 4	e♭	f♮	e♭	f♮	e♭	

Cabezon 1578	1, 3, 4	e♮	f♯	e♭	f♮	e♭	
	2	e♮	f♮	e♭	f♮	e♭	

Treatment of Ascending and Descending Lines

The practice of raising certain pitches in ascent and lowering them in
descent occasionally is encountered in the intabulations. This occurs

Ex 2.60 (a) 'Stabat Mater' I 1–2 (Milano before 1536)
(b) 'Pater noster' I 1–4 (Ochsenkun 1558)

Ex 2.61 'Stabat Mater' II 56 (Ochsenkun 1558)

within the ornamentation added to the model (see Ex 2.60) and in undecorated sections (see Ex 2.61). However, this procedure by no means was adopted universally, because these pitches also were raised in descent (see Ex 2.62).

Ex 2.62 (a) 'Pater noster' 1 4 (Milano 1546)
(b) 'Stabat Mater' 1 74–5 (Ochsenkun 1558)

Instrumentalists exercised as much flexibility in applying theoretical precepts and conventions as theorists exercised in discussing them. Individual predilection played an important role in determining specific procedures, especially in passages where more than one solution was within the bounds of normal sixteenth-century practice. Both theoretical sources and intabulations confirm that the parameters of sixteenth-century style, particularly with regard to dissonance treatment, were broad. Consequently, the subsemitone was not precluded by upper or lower voice-parts, and the removal of *mi contra fa*, nonharmonic relations, and melodic tritones depended on the level of dissonance that each musician desired in his performance. Since neither the precepts nor the conventions discussed in this book were immutable during the Renaissance, perhaps our modern view of these matters should be adjusted to accommodate these practices – practices that were commonplace in the sixteenth century.

# THREE

The German Custom

During the early and middle sixteenth century, a distinctive practice
may have existed in Germany for the performance of German music.
The first written reference to this practice was made in 1555 by the
brothers Paul and Bartholomeus Hessen. The preface to their publication *Viel feiner lieblicher stücklein Spanischer, Welscher, Englischer,
Französischer composition und tenz* (Breslau) contains a statement which
implies that the use of unnotated semitones was acceptable in the music
of other countries but was contrary to custom in German music:

> die vielfaltigen bezeichneten kreutzlen / bedeuten die Semi-
> tonien / so wider den gebrauch deutscher Musica befunden /
> wirdt darmit ihres landes gebrauch angezeiget / zu viel
> angenemer lieblicheit / wo sie recht gemacht werden. Auch
> werden an etlichen orten vitia gespürt / weil aber solches
> bein [=beim] ihrer nation also componiert und zum theil nit
> fur unrecht geacht / Auch nicht fur deutsche compositz aus-
> geben / haben wir nichts endern wollen / damit ihr art und
> das sprichwort bleibe und erhalten / Jedes land furt seinen
> eignen brauch und weise / The little cross, which frequently

> is marked [in the Hessens' edition], signifies the semitone [and is] so contrary to customary German music. With it [the little cross], [one] would show the custom of your country, to much pleasant sweetness, where they [the little crosses] would be placed properly. Also you would have noticed some imperfect places, but because such people in your country so compose, and for the most part are not regarded as wrong, [they, the little crosses] are also not designated for German compositions. We have not wanted to change [anything] in order to retain its proper nature and that [you] be left with the proverb 'Each country has its own custom and manner.' (Hessen *Viel*, preface to *tenor* part-book)

These remarks are substantiated by the notational practices exhibited in both *Viel feiner lieblicher stücklein* and the Hessens' other publication from the same year, *Etlicher gutter Teutscher und Polnischer Tenz*. Indeed, the foreign dances in *Viel feiner lieblicher stücklein* contain many notated sharps, whereas only 5 of the 155 German/Polish dances in their second volume mark the *kreutzlein*. Additional reinforcement is found in the tablatures of Hans Gerle, a Nürnberg musician, who between 1532 and 1546 intabulated both German and foreign vocal music. Gerle's intabulations further illustrate the nationalistic practices described by the Hessens and demonstrate that the practices were applied to vocal music as well as to dance music. Gerle's tablatures are perfectly suitable for a documenting of these German customs because the intabulations for both viols and lute closely approximate vocal performance. In fact, it is primarily through the study of tablatures that the specific details of this German tradition are revealed.

The normal use of semitones during the sixteenth century has been documented in the previous two chapters and must have been well known throughout Europe. Nevertheless, the tablatures of Hans Gerle do suggest that a distinct practice existed in Germany for German vocal music, that is, for music written by native composers with texts in the vernacular. As one would expect, however, Gerle does not fully substantiate the position taken by the Hessens, and his use of semitones falls into three broad categories: those pieces in which all of the cadence-notes are approached by the subtone, those in which all of

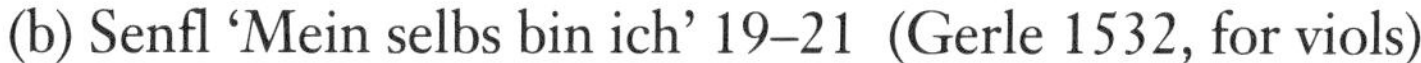

Ex 3.1 (a) Eckel 'Gesell, wis Urlaub' 7–9 (Gerle 1546, for lute)

(b) Senfl 'Mein selbs bin ich' 19–21 (Gerle 1532, for viols)

the cadence-notes are approached by the subsemitone, and those which contain a mixture of the two approaches.[1]

In the first two categories, I have been unable to explain why Gerle chose to set one text with subsemitonal *clausulae* and another with subtonal *clausulae*. No textual or musical reasons suggest themselves. This problem is particularly intriguing for those *clausulae* that employ suspension figures, because virtually all of the intabulations examined in this book use the subsemitone in these types of progressions. Example 3.1 contains two similar *clausulae*, both of which conclude main sections of the respective pieces. In 'Gesell wis Urlaub' (see Ex 3.1a), Gerle renders all of the *clausulae* with subsemitones, but in 'Mein selbs bin ich' (see Ex 3.1b), he specifies subtones. Moreover, Gerle also varies his treatment of *clausulae* when he intabulates the same piece twice, and this is one of the most fascinating aspects of Renaissance performing practice – the flexibility which pervaded the application of unnotated sharps. In Senfl's 'Patientiam muess ich han' (see Ex 3.2), Gerle designates a G♮ in the intabulation for viols but gives a G♯ in the version for lute. The freedom with which Renaissance musicians interpreted such cadential passages is well documented in the sources, especially when more than one German performer intabulated a given work. For example, Gerle desig-

Ex 3.2 Senfl 'Patientiam muess ich han' 20–1 (Gerle 1532, for viols and for lute)

nated subtones for each cadence in Senfl's 'Mein selbs bin ich,' whereas both the lutenist Sebastian Ochsenkun (1558) and the anonymous lute intabulator of Munich ms 1512 stipulated subsemitones. Obviously, a wide variety of practices existed in Germany, and the Hessens' statements reflect merely one facet of those practices.

Within the third category, Gerle seems to have organized his cadential procedure in a logical manner for at least some of the works; that is, *clausulae* at the ends of large sections carry subsemitones, but internal cadences carry subtones. His plan is seen most clearly in Senfl's 'O Herr, ich rüef dein'n Namen an' (see Ex 3.4). One might presume that the vertical constraints present in bars 24, 29, and 44 explain why Gerle chose not to incorporate subsemitones at these points. However, other *clausulae* within the work do not contain such restrictions (see bars 5, 11, 39, 48), yet these cadences were rendered with subtones. The recovery of Gerle's fascinating strategy for the overall organization of cadential procedure reveals still another side of sixteenth-century German fashion and enables present-day performers to re-create the variety of practices which existed in Germany.

Gerle's method of treating *clausulae* was, of course, not limited to German music, and his intabulations document the degree to which the practices described above were applied to foreign vocal music. His procedure in pieces such as Johannes Lupi's Dorian-mode motet

Ex 3.3 Lupi 'Spes salutis' I 19–21 (Gerle 1546, for lute)

'Spes salutis' often depended upon the nature of the part-writing, but commonly no contrapuntal reason seems to have influenced his decisions. Gerle's approach to cadences, then, was quite free and, again, took one of three forms – subtonal, subsemitonal, or suprasemitonal. Frequently, the removal of either a vertical or a linear tritone between the notes F and B produced suprasemitonal *clausulae* (see Ex 3.3). At other cadences, no vertical or linear complications were present, and Gerle often left these types of *clausulae* completely uninflected, thus illustrating the customary German practice as described by the Hessens (see Ex 3.5). Nevertheless, the subsemitone was a common feature of many *clausulae* even when this created dissonance between the parts (see Ex 3.6).

Some scholars consider Gerle's cadential procedure to lack consistency and condemn him for his non-uniform treatment of *clausulae*.[2] However, I believe that the flexibility of the theoretical framework within which Renaissance musicians operated made this diversity inevitable and that the notion of consistency is irrelevant to the issue at hand. In fact, this notion exposes the problems we have today in dealing with the bewildering array of conflicting information that survives in primary sources; furthermore, it disallows variation in musical practices. We are, after all, studying a different culture, and we

Ex 3.4 Senfl
'O Herr, ich rüef dein'n
Namen an'
(Gerle 1546, for viols)

schwer- lich auf uns ge- la- den so denk doch das wir sein ge- tauft dar- zue
schwer- lich auf uns ge- la- den so denk doch das wir sein ge- tauft dar- zue
schwer- lich auf uns ge- la- den so denk doch das wir sein ge- tauft dar- zue
schwer- lich auf uns ge- la- den so denk doch das wir sein ge- tauft dar- zue
mit Chri- sti Bluet er- kauft des- halb wöllst uns be- gna- den
mit Chri- sti Bluet er- kauft des- halb wöllst uns be- gna- den
zue mit Chri- sti Bluet er- kauft des- halb wöllst be- gna- den
mit Chri- sti Bluet er- kauft des- halb wöllst be- gna- den

Ex 3.5 Lupi 'Spes salutis' I 24–8 (Gerle 1546, for lute)

Ex 3.6 Lupi 'Spes salutis' II 21–3 (Gerle 1546, for lute)

should not use our own value systems to measure the skill with which individuals in other societies executed their craft.

 FOUR

Traditions of Pitch-Content

In recent years, the need to increase our understanding of geographically localized traditions of performance has been widely recognized by performers and scholars. Comparative study of all the sources, both vocal and instrumental, for a given motet frequently reveals that no one authoritative version of its pitch-content existed. What did exist, especially when the motet was a popular one, was a range of versions for each work. Various performers interpreted the sources at their disposal from differing perspectives, and this produced the divergent oral traditions associated with particular motets. The difficulty for us today in recovering these traditions is to determine which conventions apply to which works. Almost any piece of vocal music could be used to document this aspect of sixteenth-century musical culture, but I will focus on problematic sections in two motets, Josquin's 'Inviolata, integra et casta es' and Clemens non Papa's 'Fremuit spiritu Jesus,' before discussing the ways in which individual musicians interpreted the pitch-content of three entire motets – Josquin's 'Pater noster,' a setting of 'Absalon, fili mi' which may or may not have been composed by Josquin, and Alexander Agricola's 'Si dedero.'

Ex 4.1 'Inviolata' I 43–50

Josquin Desprez, 'Inviolata, integra et casta es'

An intriguing anomaly in one of the vocal sources of 'Inviolata' – the *Liber selectarum cantionum* (Augsburg 1520[4]) – points to the existence of two performing traditions associated with the *prima pars* of this motet. The extant intabulations document both traditions and attest to the divergent readings of this work that were known in the sixteenth century.[1] The specific problem in the 1520 print concerns the disappearance of the signature, the sign *b mollis* on B, in the closing bars of the *prima pars*. In all the voices except *tenor* II, the signature ceases to be present from bar 39. Apparently, the editor of the 1520 print felt that for four of the voices the signature easily could be omitted at this point owing to the number of vertical tritones between E and B♭, that performers would have to alter anyway (see, for instance, Ex 4.1, bar 46). But in *tenor* II, the editor had to retain the signature because B♭ is required in bar 44 to avoid the tritone with the F in the *altus*. Josquin subsequently repeated the phrase containing this B♭ three times, once identically and twice in a modified form (bars 45–7, 56–8, 58–60), and the desire to maintain the interval structure of the phrase necessitated the incorporation of B♭ and thus the retention of the signature.

For the most part, the intabulators Hans Gerle and Sebastian Ochsenkun adhered to the new signature, thereby affiliating themselves with the 1520 print. With the exception of bars 44–8 (which will be discussed presently), both these German lutenists render each B occurring after bar 39 (in voices other than *tenor* II, that is) as B♮. But for each occurrence of a B within *tenor* II (the only voice with a signature at this point; see bars 44, 46, 57, 59), Gerle and Ochsenkun indicate B♭, thus preserving the interval structure of the phrase.

However, Gerle and Ochsenkun depart radically from the 1520 version in bars 44–8. In fact, with one exception, all the intabulators stipulate B♭ for every B in this passage.[2] The logic behind this treatment stems from two factors which govern this entire section – first, the B♭ in *tenor* II of bars 44 and 46 (the melodic phrase just discussed), and second, the B♭ required for the suprasemitonal cadence in bars 44–5. Evidently, the intabulators considered it necessary to reproduce the suprasemitonal motion of the *bassus* (B♭ to A♮) in the *superius* at

Ex 4.2 Cabezón 55–6

bars 46 and 48 even though this created a tritone with the *bassus* in each case.

On the other hand, with the exception of bar 40, where all the intabulators avoid the tritone with E, Enriquez de Valderrávano stipulates B♭s throughout the closing bars of the *prima pars*, indicating that he was bound to the tradition transmitted in the extant vocal sources other than the 1520 print – a tradition in which the signature is present throughout. In essence, Antonio de Cabezón also forms part of this group, though he is inclined to raise those B♭s that occur in ascending passages (see Ex 4.2).

Thus, two performing traditions seem to have existed for 'Inviolata.' One is derived from the 1520 print and the other from the remaining vocal sources.

Clemens non Papa, 'Fremuit spiritu Jesus'

More than one performing tradition existed also for Clemens non Papa's motet 'Fremuit spiritu Jesus.' The sources for this work[3] provide an excellent example of the way in which variant signatures and sharps and flats can reveal divergent practices (see Table 4.1). For example, the use of the sign *b durum* to cancel a signature is shown in the manuscript Kassel 91. This source contains the signature B♭ in all voices except *bassus* I, in which the signature B♭ and E♭ occurs in bars 1–25. However, in bar 15 of this voice the sign *b durum* appears below the E, and this sign may have been used to cancel the signature's E♭ (see Ex 4.3). Additional support for this supposition is found in the

Table 4.1
Signatures in the *prima pars* of 'Fremuit spiritu Jesus'

Voice	B♭	B♭ & E♭
SI	all sources	—
SII	all sources (Kassel 91 & Leipzig 49 lack SII)	—
CaT	Brussels 27088 Kassel 91 1554[2] 1555[13] 1558[4] (Copenhagen 1873 lacks CaT)	Leipzig 49 (sign *b durum* below Es of bars 8 & 9)
T	all sources	—
BI	Brussels 27088 Copenhagen 1873 Kassel 91 (B♭ & E♭ 1–25, B♭ 26–end; sign *b durum* below E of bar 15)	Leipzig 49 1554[2] 1555[13] 1558[4]
BII	Kassel 91	Brussels 27088 Copenhagen 1873 Leipzig 49 1554[2] 1555[13] 1558[4]

next line of music, which simply carries the signature B♭. Hence, the original signature may have been intended to last only until bar 15.

Perhaps the most controversial passage in this motet occurs in bars 7–10 of the *prima pars* (see Ex 4.4).[4] The problems associated with this passage revolve around whether the Es should be sung as flats or as naturals or as some mixture of the two. In dealing with these problems, one might do well to bear in mind that the theoretical precepts forbidding vertical dissonance and nonharmonic relations were by no means immutable.

In Example 4.4a, the E in *bassus* II of bar 7 probably should be sung as a flat, because it is approached by leap from B♭. But how should the

Ex 4.3 'Fremuit' I, *primus bassus* 15–16

Kassel 91

Es in the *bassus* I and *contratenor* parts of bar 8 be sung? The sources of 'Fremuit' support three readings, one of which, the first to be discussed here, seems more plausible than the other two. This is Jakob Paix's keyboard intabulation (see Ex 4.4c), printed in 1589, which employs E♭ in *bassus* II and then, as frequently happens in this period, incurs a nonharmonic relation between this E♭ and the E♮s of *bassus* I and *contratenor*. As a result, each voice follows its own inner logic and produces the expected *fa–mi* clash. However, in four of the vocal sources – Leipzig 49, 1554[2], 1555[13], and 1558[4] – this solution cannot be followed, because it requires the singer to ignore the *bassus* I signature of B♭ and E♭. In Kassel 91, where this signature ceases at bar 15, one wonders why the sign *b durum*, used to cancel the signature at bar 15 (see Ex 4.5a), did not occur at bar 8 (see Ex 4.5b), especially since similar E♮ against E♭ problems are present in both passages.

Interestingly, another reading is suggested by the manuscript Brussels 27088. The *contratenor* part in this source carries a signature

Ex 4.4 'Fremuit' I 7–10

of B♭ throughout the *prima pars*, and in addition, an E♭ is marked at bar 8. *Bassus* I carries the same signature, and though no E♭ is indicated at bar 8, E♭ is marked at bar 3, where a leap from B♭ to E occurs. The jurisdiction of this sign (*b mollis* on E) may be intended to last until at least bar 8, because both Es appear on the same line of music in the manuscript. A possible solution to this passage, then, may involve solmizing the Es of *bassus* I, *bassus* II, and *contratenor* as E♭s. But this, of course, presents a new problem in bar 9. Should the As of *bassus* II and *superius* I be sung as naturals or as flats? In other words, is the dissonance between these A♮s and the E♭ of the *contratenor* an unavoidable by-product of the vocal lines' working independently of one another,

Ex 4.5 'Fremuit' I 14–16, 7–8 in Kassel 91

or is this a case in which the *mi contra fa* should be removed? If the *mi contra fa* is eliminated by singing the As as flats, then further dissonance with Ds and Gs probably would have to be removed as well, the resulting reading paralleling the one suggested many years ago by Edward Lowinsky.[5]

Another, completely different, solution, equally problematic, is contained in the vocal source Leipzig 49 and in the keyboard intabulation by Johannes Rühling (1583). In the Leipzig manuscript, E♭ is required in bar 7 of *bassus* II by the signature and by the leap from B♭. However, in bars 8 and 9 of the *contratenor* the scribe twice used the sign *b durum* to cancel the E♭s dictated by the signature (see Ex 4.6). No such cancellation of the signature occurs in *bassus* I at this point, and therefore, E♭ probably would have been sung. In fact, this is the manner in which the passage is presented in Rühling's intabulation

Ex 4.6 'Fremuit' I, *contratenor* 8–9

Leipzig 49

(see Ex 4.4b). It is possible that Rühling knew Leipzig 49, or a source very similar to it, and used it to prepare his intabulation. However, no conclusive evidence has been found to support this filial relationship or the rather unusual reading associated with that relationship. Momentary dissonant octaves, such as those discussed by Correa de Arauxo, seem within the bounds of normal Renaissance procedures, but Rühling's reading appears to push the notion of independence among voice-parts beyond the limits of credibility.

Thus, at least for bars 7–10 of this motet, three readings are suggested by extant sources. Of these readings, it is perhaps the one contained in Paix's intabulation that presents the most palatable solution to this controversial passage, given the present state of knowledge on these matters. Unfortunately, no reliable methods exist for resolving the problems associated with the reading suggested by Brussels 27088 or Rühling's intabulation.

?Josquin Desprez?, 'Absalon, fili mi'[6]

Four sources of 'Absalon, fili mi' survive: British Library, Royal 8 G vii ff 56v–58; *Selectissimae necnon familiarissimae cantiones* (Augsburg 1540[7]), no 24; Sebastian Ochsenkun, *Tabulaturbuch auff die Lauten* (Heidelberg 1558[5]), no 14, f 30; and *Tertia pars magni operis musici* (Nürnberg 1559[2]), no 10. For the most part, I will restrict my remarks to the German prints, exploring the structure of 'Absalon' as it is revealed in these prints and discussing the ways in which Ochsenkun interpreted the pitch-content of his vocal model.[7] The 1540 and 1559 editions of 'Absalon' are virtually identical, differing in that 1559[2] contains a more complete text-underlay[8] and a correction to the clef which was misplaced in the final stave of the *tenor* part of 1540[7]. The later edition also clarifies whether the E♭ at the beginning of this stave was intended to be part of a new signature or a pre-placed sign (see Ex 4.7). No change in signature occurs in 1559[2] at this point, and the desired alteration in pitch is effected by flat signs placed before those Es which require them. Presumably, the E♭ in 1540[7] never was intended to be part of a new signature but was positioned at the beginning of

Ex 4.7 *Tenor*, 1540[7] and 1559[2]

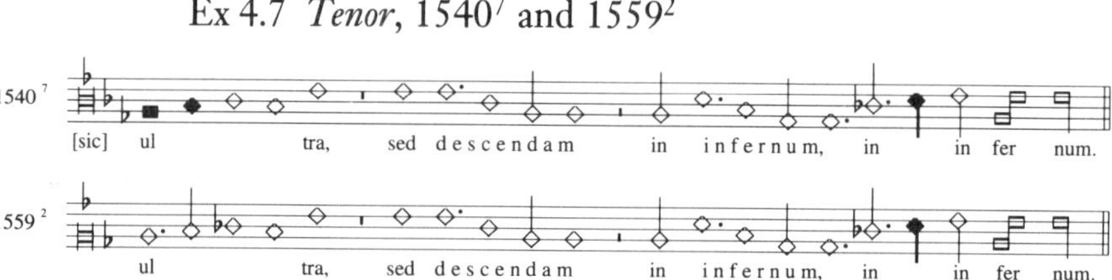

the stave in order to warn the singer of an approaching *fa* on E. Additional evidence in support of this supposition is that if the E♭ actually indicated a new signature, then the inclusion of the flat sign before the final E of the stave would have been redundant. In fact, of the three Es occurring in this stave, the only two that should bear flat signs, at least according to 1559[2] and Ochsenkun's intabulation, are the first and third; this demonstrates the localized nature of these signs.

The piece begins with a *fuga*, each voice repeating the others' solmization syllables. In this way, the voices outline and establish the species of fourths and fifths characteristic of the Lydian mode in *cantus mollis* position:

Discantus	*ut* to *fa*	Natural hexachord on C
Contratenor	*ut* to *fa*	Soft hexachord on F
Tenor	*ut* to *fa*	Natural hexachord on C
Bassus	*ut* to *fa*	Soft hexachord on F

The composer pairs the voices hexachordally, *discantus/tenor* and *contratenor/bassus*, and this coupling is retained in each subsequent *fuga*.[9] The signature of one flat associated with this mode indicates that the piece is to be sung in the scale of *b mollis*, and inherent in this hexachord system are two areas of oscillation – one, E/E♭, resulting from the E*mi*–E*fa* duality of the note of permutation and the other, A/A♭, resulting from the application of the *fa supra la* convention to the fictive hexachord on B♭ (the fictive hexachord being necessary to create the permutation to E♭):

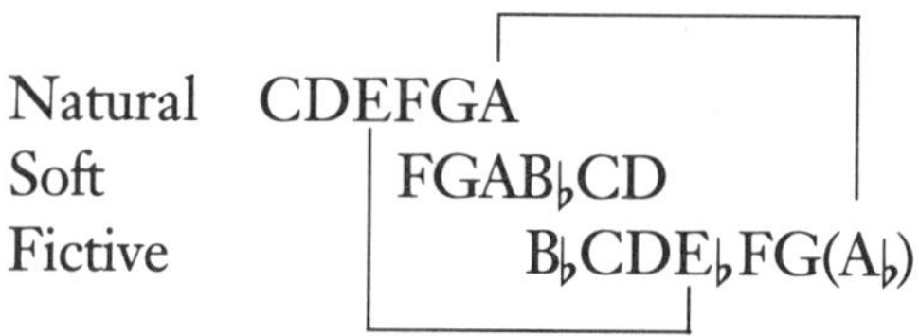

Thus, E♭ becomes an implicit part of *cantus mollis* Lydian, and A♭ an extension to the outer boundaries of the hexachord order. Within this mode, then, one would expect to encounter E♭s, and the appearance of A♭s, while extending the system to its natural limits, would not be inconceivable.[10] Indeed, a quick check of the signs occurring in this version of 'Absalon' reveals that E♭s and A♭s are the only ones designated. But how does the introduction of these signs affect modal procedure, and how does the composer use the oscillatory nature of the *cantus mollis* Lydian mode to create the *hypotyposis* figures[11] necessary for underlining the closing words of the text?

For most of the piece, the modal procedure follows normal practices. In fact, throughout 'Absalon' the music remains anchored to the structural foundations of the mode. The species of fourths and fifths are constantly being reiterated, and all the cadences, with the exception of two transitory ones on G, are either on the principal cadence-notes F and C or on the secondary note A.[12] Only in the sections bearing the words 'non vivam ultra sed descendam in infernum plorans' (bars 52–68 and their repeat in bars 69–85) does modal procedure become somewhat obscure.[13] In order to set these words appropriately, the composer utilizes the oscillatory nature of the hexachord order to prepare for the descent to inferno.

Interestingly enough, the introduction of the first specified flat sign, an E♭ (bar 52), coincides with the new text and discloses that side of the mode which tends in the flatward direction. In this case, the E♭ is essential for the avoidance of *mi contra fa* and is employed in a mimetic passage in which the *bassus*, the *dux* voice, is paired with the *contratenor*, the *comes* voice.[14] The composer uses the *comes* voice of this incomplete *fuga* to maintain an E♭ in the *concentus* while the *tenor* and *bassus* cadence on C (bar 56). Hence, the reason for the appearance of an E♭ (bar 56) at a point where no vertical dissonance is in need of correction.

Directly following this E♭ is an A♭ in the *contratenor* at bar 53 (see Ex 4.8). Two solmizations are possible for this note: a semitone extension to the fictive hexachord through the *fa supra la* convention or a mutation to yet another fictive hexachord on E♭. The *contratenor* phrase containing this A♭ originates in bar 50 as the *comes* voice of a mimetic passage which overlaps the *dux* voice of the *mimesis* just dis-

Ex 4.8 1540^7, 52–3

cussed. The phrase begins in the soft hexachord on F, and the opening leap reiterates the fourth species of fifth, thus retaining a clear link with the mode. But in order to negotiate this A♭, the singer must at some point mutate to the fictive hexachord (probably on the second G in bar 52), and the placement of a flat before the A ensures the singer's recognition of the *fa supra la* convention. The alternative solmization for this note requires the singer to mutate to a new fictive hexachord on E♭, but as further mutation in the fictive direction can be avoided, the semitone extension to the hexachord on B♭ is the preferable explanation.

The two overlapping mimetic passages draw to a close with the *comes* voice of the second passage cadencing on C (bar 60), and it is at this point that the text 'sed descendam in infernum plorans' first appears.[15] The composer depicts the descent to inferno by employing the musical-rhetorical figures *fuga* and *climax*.[16] As in previous *fugae*, he pairs the *tenor* with the *discantus* and the *bassus* with the *contratenor*. Each interlocked pair progresses downward by means of a *climax*[17] in which melodic fragments are repeated on successively lower steps. For the *tenor* and the *discantus*, this repetition entails a mutation from the natural hexachord directly to the fictive, and for the *bassus* and *contratenor*, from the soft hexachord to a fictive one on E♭. That the composer intended a new fictive hexachord to be invoked at this point is evident from the structural implications of *fugae*. In order for each voice to effect an exact duplication of the others' solmization syllables, a fictive hexachord on E♭ is necessary, and it is probably no coincidence that in both 1540[7] and 1559[2] the employment of this fictive element corresponds with the text 'in infernum.' The *bassus*' A♭ in bar 66 thus is accommodated easily in theory and practice by this fictive solmization.

Combining this *fuga* with the descending *climax* results in the creation of a chain of fifths – C, F, B♭, E♭, and A♭.[18] Consequently, the composer's imaginative setting of the text makes full use of the oscillatory nature of the hexachord system while allowing him to retain modal control. His unambiguous employment of the species of *cantus mollis* Lydian throughout this section and his adherence to the structural foundations of the mode demonstrate his mastery of the modal medium. Now that the essential structure of the pitch-content has been established, the details of interpreting signs either specified or editorially added must be examined.

Ochsenkun's intabulation of 'Absalon, fili mi' furnishes a precise view of how a contemporary performer interpreted a vocal source. But in order to make a meaningful comparison between this intabulation and its model, we must determine the source from which Ochsenkun worked. The number and nature of the surviving vocal sources for 'Absalon' limit the *stemma* to two branches – Royal 8 comprising one branch and 1540[7]/1559[2] the other. Of these, the 1559[2] print first appeared the year after Ochsenkun's *Tabulaturbuch* was published and therefore immediately can be eliminated as the model. The British Library manuscript also can be dismissed, as it would have been inaccessible to Ochsenkun, unless, of course, he travelled to England and came across the manuscript there.[19] But even if Ochsenkun never had the opportunity to see Royal 8 itself, the possibility cannot be ruled out that sources identical to it may have circulated in northern Europe during the middle of the sixteenth century. Additional grounds exist, however, for rejecting this version as the one employed by Ochsenkun.

The differences between Royal 8 and 1540[7] confirm the hypothesis that the Royal 8 version probably was unknown to Ochsenkun. Two melodic and two harmonic variants establish this premise. In bars 24–5 of the *discantus* and in bar 45 of the *contratenor*, Ochsenkun follows the melodic structure of 1540[7] (see Ex 4.9). The two harmonic variants involve pitches that are lowered in one vocal source but not in the other. 1540[7] contains A♭s in bars 53 and 70 of the *contratenor* and

Ex 4.9 Variants in the sources

Ex 4.10 Variants in Ochsenkun

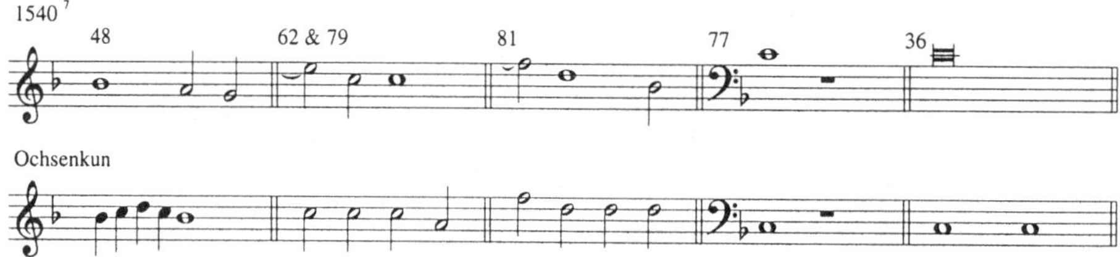

an E♮ in bar 51 of the *tenor*, all of which are present in the intabulation (see Ex 4.9).[20] Therefore, it is probable that Ochsenkun prepared his transcription either from a copy of this print or from a source very similar to it.

A number of discrepancies between Ochsenkun's intabulation and the 1540 print, however, suggest that another source almost identical to 1540^7 once existed. Certain variants occur in passages that contain no ornamentation in the voices concerned (see Ex 4.10). These variants are minor, and although they might justify the belief in a lost source, their existence does not invalidate the possibility that 1540^7 was Ochsenkun's model. The similarities between the intabulation and 1540^7, the geographic proximity of their origins, and the fact that the 1540^7 version remained current in Germany after the publication of Ochsenkun's *Tabulaturbuch* suggest a filial relationship between the sources.

In transcribing 'Absalon,' Ochsenkun incorporated all of the flat signs specified in his model, thereby furnishing a meticulous view of the localized nature of these signs. In fact, his intabulation provides further documentation of how the vocal lines' following their own inner logic produces nonharmonic relations. Example 4.11 contains a striking situation in which the *discantus* employs an A♮ that is imme-

Ex 4.11 1540[7] and Ochsenkun, 53

53

vi-   vam

[-li]

tra,   ul-

vi-   vam

diately followed by an A♭ in the *contratenor*. Each part proceeds unhampered by the other,[21] the resultant clash being retained by Ochsenkun. Occasionally, ornamentation becomes a vehicle for the creation of dissonant relationships where none occur naturally in the model (see Ex 4.12). The decoration added to the *discantus* in bar 22 includes a B♮ which conflicts with the following B♭ in the *contratenor*, and in bar 56 the forward direction of the subsemitone to F appears to be more important than the maintaining of unity with either the preceding or the following E♭.

A remarkable use of sharps and flats colours Ochsenkun's efforts to effect a smooth transition to bar 69 (where the repeat of bars 52–68 begins) (see Ex 4.13). He perceives the first half of bar 68 as belonging 'harmonically' to the preceding material and the second as belonging to that which follows. The ornamentation of the *tenor*'s A–G includes the subsemitones for C (B♮) and G (F♯), but in the second half of the bar, Ochsenkun prepares the way for the *bassus'* E♭ through a decoration of the *contratenor*'s leap from C to G which contains B♭, E♭, and F.[22]

In addition to clarifying dissonant relationships which modern ears

Ex 4.12 1540⁷ and Ochsenkun, 22–3, 56–8
22 23 56 57 58
-sa- lon fi- li non vi- vam ul-
[-sa-] lon non vi- vam ul-
-li mi Ab sa non vi- vam ul-
[ul-] tra, non ul-

Ex 4.13 1540[7] and Ochsenkun, 68–9

might be tempted to remove editorially, and demonstrating how these can be created through embellishment, Ochsenkun supplies details of modal procedure at cadence points. Cadential articulation is reinforced by the introduction of the subsemitone at all points where the subsemitone does not occur naturally (except, of course, suprasemitonal cadences) and, as we have seen, at other points where the undecorated model prohibits its employment.[23] All cadences on C, then, are approached by B♮, and those on G by F♯. Repeatedly, the strong subsemitonal pull to the *epidiapente* proved particularly attractive to Ochsenkun, and the embellishment of the opening *fuga* exemplifies this aspect of his modal procedure. The frequent oscillation between *Bmi* and *Bfa* created by the introduction of this subsemitone in cadential and noncadential passages pervades the intabulation.[24] Thus, the performer can articulate the infrastructure of the work by employing devices that were the common property of all the musicians of the period, and this shows just how much control the performer had over the final shaping of the music in both harmonic and melodic content.

Josquin Desprez, 'Pater noster'

Even without a study of filial relationships between intabulations and vocal sources, important traditions of pitch-content can be identified within the extant intabulations of specific motets. The intabulations of Josquin's setting of the prayer 'Pater noster' exemplify two such traditions. One is found in the work of the famous Italian virtuoso Francesco da Milano, and the other in the work of the German lutenist Simon Gintzler, who was in the employ of Christoforo Mudrazzo (1512–78), cardinal and prince-bishop of Trent. Their intabulations show us how two performers active in Italy during the 1540s added sharps and flats to the motet. Both musicians operated within the theoretical framework that survives from the middle of the century but applied theoretical principles in different ways. In fact, their readings present divergent practical solutions for modern performers and editors to emulate. And as we have learned to expect, neither musician was consistent in his approach, the theoretical tradition being flexible enough to accommodate individual predilections.

'Pater noster' is in Dorian mode transposed to G, and Josquin clearly establishes the species of fifth characteristic of this mode at the beginning of the motet, reiterating the species throughout the work. The piece is sung in the scale of *b mollis*, and the note of permutation, E, enables the music to oscillate between E♮ and E♭. The use of E♭, however, does not violate the integrity of the mode, for modal identity is maintained by other means, such as species and cadences. Moreover, the oscillation to E♭ is an integral part of all *b mollis* modes, especially because it frequently is employed to avoid the tritone between B♭ and E. This oscillation should be viewed as an important part of modal procedure which helps to shape the sense of mode in polyphonic music sung in the scale of *b mollis*. The cadences chosen by Josquin predominantly adhere to the structural foundations of G Dorian (G and D), with occasional *clausulae* on A (four times), B♭ (twice), C (once), and F (once). These cadence-notes call for the addition of F♯, C♯, and B♮ to create approaches to the ultimate notes of the *clausulae* through the closest imperfect intervals. Once again, these alterations do not violate the integrity of the mode; instead, they are localized modifications designed to produce a specific vertical progression.

With one exception, the use of G♯ at a cadence on A, the sharps and flats listed above, that is, E♭, F♯, C♯, and B♮, are the only ones added by Francesco and Gintzler. However, each musician creates a distinctive aural image for the listener, the individuality of their musical personalities being revealed most clearly in their interpretations of cadences, *sol fa sol* progressions, repeated phrases, and mimetic material.

Francesco renders most of the cadences subsemitonally unless vertical considerations take precedence.[25] For example, cadences on D preceded by doubled Cs are subtonal (ɪ 82; ɪɪ 16), but when the penultimate *concentus* contains both B♭ and E, the E is lowered and a suprasemitonal cadence is formed (ɪ 46). The main exceptions to this practice concern *clausulae* on A, which are naturally suprasemitonal, and three cadences on G that remain subtonal. No compelling vertical impediment exists for two of the G *clausulae* (ɪ 59; ɪɪ 74), and in the third case (ɪɪ 19) no impediment is present at all. Perhaps the custom discussed in relation to Germany in the preceding chapter occasionally was practised in Italy as well. Francesco does treat one of the A cadences, however, with what might appear to be considerable artistic licence, approaching the cadence-note by the major sixth $^{G\sharp}_{B\natural}$ rather than the $^{G}_{B\flat}$ sonority one would expect (ɪ 39). In Chapter 2, I suggested a reason for this procedure. Francesco may have wanted to create a particularly strong cadence at this structurally important point – one that would draw attention to itself through its unusual nature. On first hearing, another *clausula* (ɪ 15) also may seem to be outside normal mid-sixteenth-century procedures, but Francesco's approach to the cadence-note C from B♮ simply followed the theorist Lanfranco's recognition that in the scale of *b mollis* cadences on C could carry the *diesis* on the penultimate note.[26]

Simon Gintzler, on the other hand, treats some of these *clausulae* in a manner remarkably different from that of Francesco, particularly those cadences on D and C.[27] The *clausula* on C (ɪ 15) is subtonal, but the majority of the cadences on D are rendered either subtonally or suprasemitonally. In only three cases, does he create subsemitonal cadences (ɪ 32; ɪɪ 43, 46), whereas Francesco employed the subsemitone eight times. One of the reasons for this is that the two musicians intabulated contrasting versions of the piece. In the *secunda pars* (48–9,

57–8), Francesco's exemplar contained the cadential figure

in the *quinta vox*, but Gintzler's exemplar reproduced the line as

The subsemitone was required, of course, for the suspension figure in Francesco's model. But the melodic line B♭–C–D in Gintzler's source makes the cadence less prominent and less in need of a subsemitonal approach, especially when the addition of a C♯ would create a linear augmented second with B♭.

Of Gintzler's subtonal cadences on D, three (I 82; II 13, 16) result from part-writing which contains doubled Cs, but the other five (I 36, 97; II 31, 62, 65) are not constrained to the same degree, as only the note G appears in the *concentus*. However, in four of these five cadences, the E is doubled, preventing a suprasemitonal approach to the cadence-note. Nonetheless, at other points suprasemitonal cadences on D do occur in Gintzler, but they always arise when it is necessary to avoid vertical dissonance between E and B♭ (I 42, 46; II 49, 52, 55, 58).

Francesco and Gintzler differ in other cadential procedures as well. In 6–5–1 melodic progressions at cadences on G (I 52–3, 100–1), Francesco incorporates E♭ (E♭–D–G), but Gintzler uses E♮. Similarly, the two musicians disagree on whether or not to raise the third at cadences on A. Francesco inflects the C whenever it is present in the sonority, while Gintzler leaves it in the lowered form. They both, however, tend to raise thirds at cadences on G and D unless some impediment (doubled Bs and Fs) prevents them from doing so. Two of these passages (I 56–9, 70–2) are particularly instructive, for they demonstrate how the introduction of the raised third could control the sonority of an entire phrase. Both musicians raise the third at the cadence on G in I 56 and maintain this B♮ for the next three bars, even though in bar 57 B♭ is implied in nine vocal sources.[28] The scribes of these sources mark flat signs before the following E, the next note of the *sexta pars*, demonstrating that the preceding note was presumed by them to be a B♭. In I 70–2, a passage which does not contain standard cadential part-writing, Francesco and Gintzler were so attracted to the sonority of the raised third above the *finalis* that

Gintzler incorporated B♮ on the last two notes of the phrase, and Francesco introduced it two bars earlier.

Francesco quite frequently felt the strong subsemitonal pull to the *finalis* of the mode, even when the note G was not part of a cadence but was embedded in *sol fa sol* progressions within phrases (I 20, 24, 31, 51–2, 73–5, 96–7; II 47). However, only twice did he employ the semitone in other similar progressions, notably those involving the *repercussio* D (I 76–7) and the line C–B♭–C (I 70–1). Moreover, Francesco did not add the semitone to these types of progressions every time the opportunity arose (I 35, 54–5; II 50, 53, 56), and this shows us today just how flexibly we could and probably should treat these passages. Gintzler, on the other hand, rarely incorporated the semitone at these points, simply adding an F♯ to two *sol fa sol* progressions (I 31, 51–2).

The strong subsemitonal pull to the structural foundations of the mode (G and D) is also present in the melodic repetitions at the opening of the work. The *quinta vox*'s line G–G–G–F, its repetition, and its restatement in the *superius* as D–D–D–C all are rendered with semitones in Francesco's intabulation. However, as with the *sol fa sol* progressions, Gintzler is less inclined to be attracted to this sort of semitonal motion and reserves the semitone exclusively for bar 6, treating each repetition differently. And yet in another passage containing repeated material (II 46–58), it is Gintzler who is consistent in his application of unnotated signs and not Francesco (see Ex 2.59).

Josquin set the *tenor* and *altus* canonically in both parts of the motet, the *prima pars* containing a canon at the fifth and the *secunda pars* a canon at the unison. In the *secunda pars*, both lutenists repeat the solmization syllables of the *dux* exactly, not even specifying raised thirds at cadences. But in the *prima pars*, Francesco added a number of signs to one voice but not to the other. This mainly occurred at *clausulae*, and in two passages (I 14/17, 66/69) he incorporated the raised third in the *comes*, although no *clausula* was present in the *dux*. Similarly, Francesco treated a *sol fa sol* progression semitonally in the *dux* but tonally in the *comes*, probably because vertical impediments above and below the *comes* prevented him from adding the semitone (see I 24/27). Vertical impediments controlled Francesco's procedure at cadences as well, and in I 36/39 and 94/97 he was forced to add sharps to only one of the voices. Gintzler, however, chose for the most part to retain the intervallic integrity of the canon, making only one alteration (I 46). It would appear as if the sanctity of the intervals of a canon could be broken when compelling musical reasons warranted the addition of sharps, or flats for that matter, to one of the voices but not the other.

In their interpretations of this motet, both musicians exercised complete control over its pitch-content and presented the listener with separate but equally acceptable versions of the work. Because we do not know what Josquin's own predilections might have been, we are faced today with what I regard as the rather pleasant prospect of performing contrasting interpretations of the motet's pitch-content. This brings us in touch with the sixteenth century in a very real way, for divergent performing traditions are exactly what existed at that time. We should, in my view, begin reflecting these traditions in our modern performances, especially when, as will be seen next, a work is transmitted to us in two different modes.

Alexander Agricola, 'Si dedero'

No single concept of polyphonic modality existed for sixteenth-century practising musicians, and the notion of what constituted normal modal procedure varied widely among Renaissance performers. For example, Alexander Agricola's motet 'Si dedero' demonstrates that the *tetrardus* mode could contain many unnotated signs, including B♭, E♭, F♯, C♯, and G♯, and could be transformed into G-*protus* through the addition of B♭ as a signature. The surviving sources of the motet, both vocal and instrumental, attest to this, for in some of them the piece was notated in the scale of *b durum* (indicating hypomixolydian mode), and in others at least one of the voices was notated in the scale of *b mollis* (indicating hypodorian mode on G).[29] The intabulations of the work, in addition to revealing lost vocal sources, confirm this hypothesis and show that 'Si dedero' indeed was known in these two modal guises. Fourteen vocal sources and three lute intabulations preserve the piece in hypomixolydian mode, whereas five vocal sources and two keyboard intabulations transmit the work in G-hypodorian (see Table 4.2).[30] In each of these categories, the signs present in the sources define the

Table 4.2
Signatures and mode in 'Si dedero'

		Hypomixolydian	*G-Hypodorian*	
Signature:	*Superius*	♮	♮	♮
	Tenor	♮	♮	♭
	Contra	♮	♭	♭
Source:		Bologna Q 17	Bologna Q 16[a]	Kotter
		Bologna Q 18	Florence 178	Sicher
		Brussels 11239	Rome 2856	
		Copenhagen 1848	Vatican XIII 27	
		Florence 27	Verona DCCLVII	
		Florence 229		
		Munich 3154		
		Paris Vm^7 676		
		Paris 1597		
		Saint Gall 462		
		Saint Gall 463		
		Segovia		
		1501		
		1538^9		
		Spinacino		
		Capirola		
		Newsidler		

[a] The flat sign for the signature is placed only on the second and third
lines of music.

sense of mode for each musician, and the intabulations illustrate the
range of sharps and flats that may be employed in mode eight.

Although no sharps are notated in the vocal sources, these sources
do contain a number of flats in both the hypomixolydian and G-
hypodorian readings of the motet. The hypomixolydian sources mark
flats on the notes F, B, and E, and in some of these sources the flats
were specified to ensure that the singer selected the correct hexachord.
The reading in Florence 27, for example, includes two flats in the *contra*
part, one pre-placed at the beginning of bar 16 but governing the B of
bar 18 (see Ex 4.14b), and the other governing the F of bar 8 but placed
one note early (see Ex 4.14a). In bar 8, the flat indicates the location of
fa, and this instructs the singer to solmize the phrase using the natural
(C) hexachord. Without *b molli*s, a singer might mistakenly begin this

Ex 4.14 'Si dedero' (a) *contra* 7–10 (b) *contra* 14–20

rising line on *ut* in the soft (F) hexachord, introducing an unnecessary B♮ into mode eight. The flat in bar 16 also indicates the location of *fa*, but in this case it is there for the opposite reason; that is, it is there to make certain that the singer actually introduced B♭ into the sonority. Consequently, the sign *b mollis* is pre-placed at the beginning of the *deductio*, and this ensures that singers will mutate to the soft (F) hexachord rather than the hard (G) hexachord.

Three of the hypomixolydian vocal sources (Brussels 11239, Copenhagen 1848, and Paris Vm⁷ 676) specify an E♭ in bar 33 of the *contra* (see Ex 4.15). In notating this bar, the scribes must have presumed that the leap to the E♭ was from a B♭. However, apart from the flat sign before the E, nothing in these three manuscripts tells performers to incorporate this B♭: the *contra* is notated in the scale of *b durum*, with no flat sign appearing earlier in the part, and the horizontal/vertical context does not require a flatward modification at this point. Perhaps this E♭ was introduced *causa pulchritudinis* (for the sake of beauty) and was intended to control the entire passage, that is, to govern all of the Bs in bars 32–3 and the E in bar 33, pushing these notes in a flatward direction (documentary support for this suggestion will be given below when the Capirola intabulation is discussed).[31]

Ex 4.15 'Si dedero' 31–5

Ex 4.16 'Si dedero' (a) 10–14 (b) 31–5 (c) 53–5

The intabulations which preserve the motet in hypomixolydian mode furnish a precise view of how three musicians, Francesco Spinacino (1507), Vincenzo Capirola (ca 1517), and Hans Newsidler (1536), defined the character of the *tetrardus* mode in relation to 'Si dedero.' According to these sources, three places occur in the motet where flats are appropriate to a reading in the scale of *b durum* (bars 11–12, 32–3, 54; see Ex 4.16).[32] In one of these places (bar 11), a variant present in the Newsidler intabulation (and the two keyboard intabulations to be discussed later), but not present in the surviving vocal sources, eliminates the need for removing *mi contra fa* (see Ex 4.16a). Apparently, some of the intabulators worked from a version of the motet which, instead of a B, had a D below the *superius'* F. As a result, Newsidler did not have to contend with dissonance at this point and, in fact, chose not to add any flats to the motet. He did, however, include a number of F♯s in both cadential and noncadential passages. Every cadence on G carried the subsemitone (bars 35, 53, 76), and Newsidler felt the strong subsemitonal pull to the final of the mode even when the note F was not part of a cadential passage (*superius* bar 5, *tenor* bar 71, and *contra* bar 53).

Spinacino and Capirola applied sharps and flats much more liberally than Newsidler. Spinacino added B♭s in two places: bar 11 of the *contra* to avoid *mi contra fa* with the F of the *superius*, maintaining the B♭ in the *deductio* until bar 13 (but omitting the B in bar 12, thereby avoiding a dissonant octave with the B♮ of the *superius*; see Ex 4.16a); and bar 54 of the *contra* to avoid the linear tritone with the following F (see Ex 4.16c). In addition, each cadence on G carried the subsemitone, as did the cadence on A in bar 73. Capirola, Spinacino's contemporary, added far more sharps and flats, and his reading demonstrates just how freely some musicians treated *tetrardus* modes in the early sixteenth century. Like Spinacino, he added B♭ to the *contra* in bar 11 and maintained the sonority throughout the *deductio* (but omitted the B in bar 13), and this caused him to lower the B of the *superius* in bar 12 (in order to avoid the dissonant octave which would have occurred otherwise). Furthermore, Capirola must have prepared his intabulation from a vocal source which contained a flat sign before the E of bar 33 (that is, a source similar to Brussels 11239, Copenhagen 1848, or Paris Vm⁷ 676, discussed above), for all of the Bs in bars 32–3 (except the *tenor's* B in bar 33, which Capirola omits) and the E in bar 33 carry flats (see Ex 4.16b).[33] He incorporated many of the same sharps as Newsidler and Spinacino, rendering all of the cadences on G and the one on A in bar 73 subsemitonally. And as with other intabulators, Capirola felt the strong subsemitonal pull to the final of the mode outside cadential passages, particularly at bars 19 and 71, and he took what may seem on first hearing to be the somewhat unusual step of creating the effect of a cadence on A in bar 5. This is, however, not such an odd procedure, for Capirola simply raises the first three notes of the *superius* to G♯ in preparation for bar 5, where the *contra* and *superius* open to a perfect consonance. He merely follows the recommendations of those theorists who advocate approaching all perfect consonances from the closest imperfect interval, regardless of whether or not the passage forms part of a cadence.[34]

It would appear, then, that the *tetrardus* mode could accommodate a wide variety of sharps and flats, the usage varying according to individual taste and the vocal source from which the intabulator worked. The signs added by Newsidler, Spinacino, and Capirola should be regarded as localized modifications which do not alter the basic character of the mode. They are, in fact, supplemental to the mode and reflect the intabulators' desire to enhance certain melodic progressions through the application of well-known principles. If one wanted to change radically or indeed transform the character of the *tetrardus* mode, one would have to follow procedures like those encountered in the sources of 'Si dedero' which preserve the motet in G-*protus*; that is, one would have to notate at least some of the voice-parts in the scale of *b mollis*.

The G-*protus* sources present two main signature traditions for the motet (see Table 4.2), the two keyboard intabulations by Johannes Kotter (ca 1512–32) and Fridolin Sicher (ca 1512–21) pointing to lost vocal sources which must have had both the *contra* and the *tenor* notated in the scale of *b mollis*. In fact, it is mainly through these B♭ signatures that we are able to establish the existence of a G-*protus* reading in the sixteenth century. In Kotter's intabulation, all of the Bs in the *tenor* and *contra* (except bar 54 of the *contra*) are rendered as flats, with no E♭s being required because the E in bar 33 is omitted. Interestingly, all of the Bs in the *superius* remain B♮s (the problem this creates will be discussed below). Sicher follows a similar pattern, notating all of the Bs in the *tenor* and most of the Bs in the *contra* as B♭s (except *contra* bars 8, 12, 13, 27–9, 54). Unlike Kotter, however, he renders the Es of the *contra* in bars 33–5 as flats. In the *superius*, most of the Bs remain unaltered, save those in bars 32–3, which are lowered. In both sources, the subsemitonal pull to G was strong, particularly for Kotter,[35] and each performer incorporated the subsemitone at the cadence on A in bar 73. But only Sicher included a cadential C♯ in bar 9.

If no alterations were undertaken in the *superius*, as in the Kotter intabulation, the incorporation of B♭ in the signatures of the two lower voices would produce simultaneous dissonant octaves with the upper part in four places (bars 12, 32, 44, 68). Although Kotter did not remove these dissonances, Sicher eliminated them in bar 12 by raising the *contra* to B♮ (not suggested in the surviving vocal sources) and in bar 32 by lowering the *superius* (paralleling the reading contained in Bologna Q16 and Verona DCCLVII). Consequently, Sicher avoided *mi contra fa* in two of the three places where the dissonance was particularly notice-able. However, in bar 44 the dissonant octave was of such a short duration that obviously he decided to incur a *punto intenso contra remisso*. In comparison, Kotter's tablature is problematic. I offer no explanation for Kotter's approach; of course, he actually may have intended to retain all of these dissonances, but this, at least according to our present knowledge, seems unlikely. As mentioned earlier in this chapter, momentary dissonant octaves that appear in passing seem appropriate to vocal polyphony, but the clashes in bars 12, 32, and 68 really are outside the normal Renaissance penchant for dissonance. Nonetheless, despite these vexatious passages, the *superius* does con-tain twelve other Bs which are not troublesome, and all of these remain unaltered in both keyboard intabulations.

It would seem that just as the *tetrardus* mode admitted so many B♭s, G-*protus* accommodated a similar number of B♮s. *B durum* performed an important function in transposed *protus*. It was required for cadences on C (bars 13, 31, 63) and other approaches to C (bars 20, 44–5, 69, 70), for *sol fa sol* progressions (C–B♮–C) sung with a semitone (bar 29), for passages outlining F♯–B either linearly (bar 68) or vertically (bar 71), and for avoiding the chromatic line B♭–A–G♯–A at cadences on A (bar 72). One should expect to find, then, *b durum* occurring frequently in G-*protus*. *B durum* does not destroy the fundamental character of the mode, for the principles governing contrapuntal progressions demand the addition of a large number of sharps and flats to the vocal parts. In my view, these alterations do not change the basic character of the mode; on the contrary, they helped create the sense of mode for Renaissance musicians. Recovery of the precise notes which sixteenth-century musicians performed not only reveals the wide variety of practices which constituted normal modal procedure but also allows our aural image of Renaissance polyphony to be shaped by some of the greatest performers of the age.

CONCLUSION

The basic problem for sixteenth-century musicians dealing with the application of unnotated sharps and flats to the vocal music of the century was ambiguous notation, and it remains a problem for us today. The issue was discussed by theorists, such as Pietro Aaron, and the great temporal distance that separates us from them only compounds the difficulty we face in recovering the principles that governed sixteenth-century practices. We are, of course, outside the culture, yet somehow we must reconstruct the practices, using our reconstruction as the factual basis for solving musical problems articulated in the treatises. As we have seen, one ignores intabulations at the risk of overlooking important contemporary evidence.

Perhaps now we should be thinking in terms of a range of solutions to a particular problem rather than in terms of a single, definitive solution. Owing to the nature of surviving vocal sources, the composer's intention for a specific passage often is lost to us, but the intentions of other musicians are not. Through our knowledge of these divergent approaches, we should strive to establish the boundaries of sixteenth-century practices and to understand the various traditions that existed within those boundaries. Then we should reflect the breadth of those practices in our modern performances and editions. A motet by Josquin Desprez, for example, never was a fixed entity, and its text probably cannot be established in one critical edition alone, for the surviving sources are merely the artefacts of what was once a living, constantly changing tradition. German, French, Italian, and Spanish sources of Josquin's music represent the way his music was known in those countries. Intabulations from these regions record the manners in which various musicians realized the pitch-content of the sources from which they worked. The necessary editing was carried out by performers who probably were totally familiar with the musical traditions of their own geographical areas, or at least by musicians who would have been more familiar with those traditions than any of us today ever could hope to be. Their intabulations are transmitted to us as part of the legacy through which we attempt to know the past.

In our efforts to reconstruct sixteenth-century performing practices, I suggest that we consider adopting the period's traditions of pitch-content in a very real fashion, adding sharps and flats to vocal works following the practices found in intabulations.[1] In choosing intabulations as models, we can be assured of aligning ourselves with customs that existed at a time when the vocal work certainly was part of a living musical tradition. Tablatures richly detail these traditions, affording us the opportunity of studying solmization and modal procedure from the viewpoint of performers rather than from the perspective of theorists. The information gleaned from intabulations, as given in Chapters 2 to 4 and supported by the discussion of theoretical literature in Chapter 1, may be applied to vocal sources in several ways. One might present the pitch-content of a work as it was conceived by an individual intabulator, emulating a reading known to have been produced by a sixteenth-century editor. Or one might conflate sources – but here we must decide whether or not conservative applications of sharps and flats should be mixed with more liberal practices (for example, conflating Simon Gintzler's version of 'Pater noster' with that of Francesco da Milano or Hans Newsidler's realization of 'Si dedero' with that of Vincenzo Capirola). A third possibility, the only one available to us when no intabulations of a vocal composition survive, simply involves working within the boundaries of sixteenth-century practices to create a reading which, although it cannot reflect any particular source or sources, follows the customs of the period in a general way, allowing us to place our intuitive responses, whether conservative or liberal, within the musical culture of the period. In other words, intabulations reveal the diversity with which theoretical doctrine was translated into actual practice. After all, a discussion of every procedure encountered in the intabulations has been found in theoretical treatises – literature, I might emphasize, which primarily treats vocal music. Both singers and instrumentalists worked within the same theoretical framework, and this makes the notion that few sharps and flats were added to vocal music in the sixteenth century no longer tenable, especially if one acknowledges that intabulations may very well be a reliable guide to the sound of vocal music.

APPENDIX

?Josquin Desprez?
'Absalon, fili mi'
1540[7] no 24

35
40
Quis det ut mo- ri- ar pro- te pro-
fi- li mi, Fi- li mi Ab- sa- lon, Quis det ut mo- ri-
mi Ab- sa- lon, Ab- sa- lon fi- li mi, Quis det ut mo-
lon, Ab- sa-lon fi- li mi, fi- li mi, Quis det ut mo- ri- ar pro- te, quis det ut mo-
45
50
te, non vi- vam
ar pro- te, Fi- li mi Ab- sa- lon, Ab- sa- lon fi- li
[3]
ri- ar pro- te, fi- li mi Ab- sa- lon, non vi- vam ul- tra, ul-
ri- ar pro- te, fi- li mi Ab- sa- lon, non vi- vam
55
60
ul- tra, non vi- vam ul- tra, sed de- scen- dam sed de- scen-
mi, non vi- vam ul- tra, sed de- scen- dam in in-
tra, non vi- vam ul- tra, sed de- scen- dam in in- fer- num,
ul- tra, ul- tra, sed de- scen- dam in in- fer-

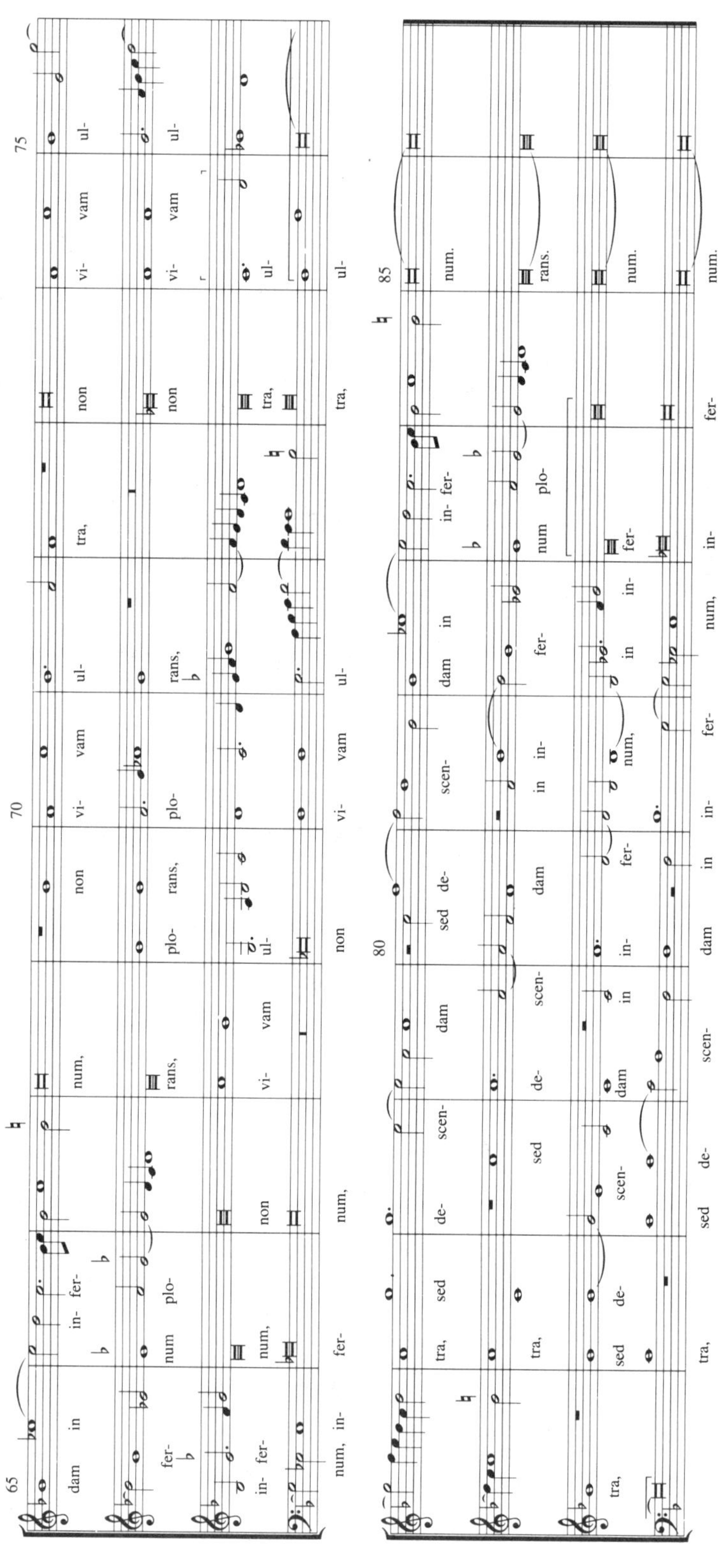
65
70
75
80
85
dam in in- fer- num, in-
fer- num plo- rans, non plo- rans,
in- fer- num, non
num, in- fer- num
sed de- scen- dam
tra, sed de- scen- dam
tra, sed de- scen- dam in in-
tra, sed de- scen- dam in in- fer-
non vi- vam ul-
plo- rans, vi- vam ul-
tra, ul- vam vi- vam ul-
num, non vi- vam
dam in in- fer-
scen- dam in in- fer-
in in- num, in- fer-
fer- in in- num, in-
num. rans. num. num.
non vi- vam ul-
non vi- vam ul-
tra, tra,

Josquin Desprez
'Pater noster'
1558[4] no 2

(In the superscript signs, Francesco's reading appears on the left and Gintzler's on the right)

PRIMA PARS
Superius
Altus
Quinta
Tenor
Sexta
Bassus

fi- at, fi- at, fi- at vo- lun- tas tu- a, sic- ut in
Fi- at vo- lun- tas tu- a,
a, fi- at, fi- at vo- lun- tas tu- a, sic- ut in cae- lo et in ter- ra,
Fi- at vo- lun- tas tu- a, sic- ut in
fi- at, fi- at vo- lun- tas tu- a, sic- ut in cae- lo et in ter- ra,
Fi- at vo- lun- tas tu- a, fi- at vo- lun- tas tu- a, sic- ut in cae- lo et in ter- ra,
cae- lo et in ter- ra. Pa- nem no- strum quo- ti- di- a- num,
sic- ut in cae- lo et in ter- ra.
sic- ut in cae- lo et in ter- ra. Pa- nem no- strum
cae- lo et in ter- ra. Pa- nem no- strum
sic- ut in cae- lo et in ter- ra. Pa- nem no- strum quo- ti- di- a- num,
sic- ut in cae- lo et in ter- ra. Pa- nem no- strum pa- nem no- strum

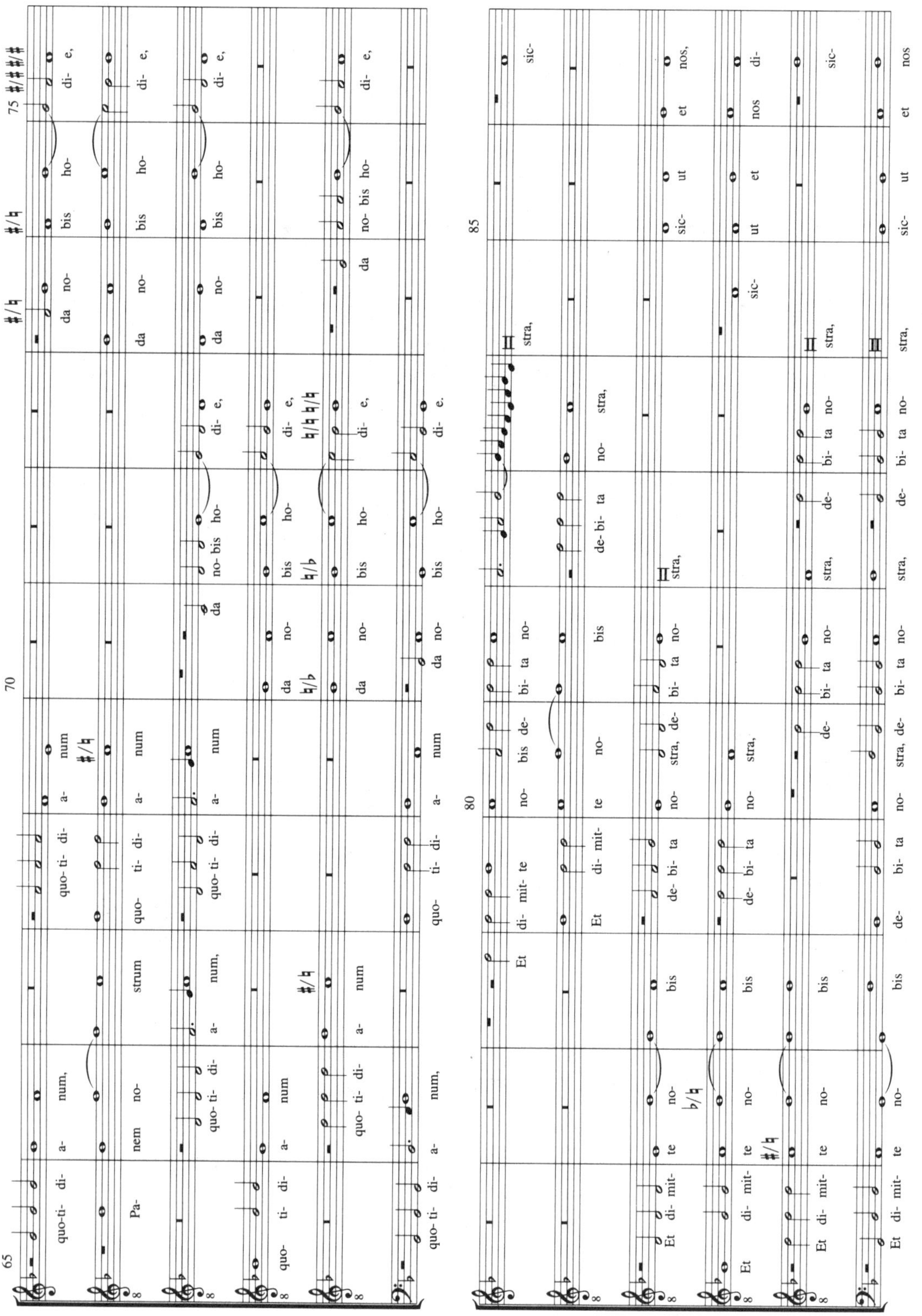
65
70
75
quo-ti- di- a- num, quo-ti- di- a- num da no- bis ho- di- e,
Pa- nem no- strum quo- ti- di- a- num da no- bis ho- di- e,
quo-ti- di- a- num, quo-ti- di- a- num da no-bis ho- di- e, da no- bis ho- di- e,
quo- ti- di- a- num da no- bis ho- di- e,
quo- ti- di- a- num da no- bis ho- di- e, da no- bis ho- di- e,
quo-ti- di- a- num, quo- ti- di- a- num da no- bis ho- di- e.
80
85
Et di- mit- te no- bis de- bi- ta no- stra, sic-
Et di- mit- te no- bis de- bi- ta no- stra,
Et di- mit- te no- bis de- bi- ta no- stra, de- bi- ta no- stra, sic- ut et nos,
Et di- mit- te no- bis de- bi- ta no- stra, sic- ut et nos di-
Et di- mit- te no- bis de- bi- ta no- stra, de- bi- ta no- stra, sic-
Et di- mit- te no- bis de- bi- ta no- stra, de- bi- ta no- stra, sic- ut et nos

ut et nos di- mit- ti- mus de- bi- to- ri- bus no- stris.
sic- ut et nos di- mit- ti- mus de- bi- to- ri- bus no-
sic- ut et nos di- mit- ti- mus de- bi- to- ri- bus no- stris, de- bi- to-
mit- ti- mus de- bi- to- ri- bus no- stris.
ut et nos di- mit- ti- mus de- bi- to- ri- bus no- stris.
di- mit- ti- mus de- bi- to- ri- bus no- stris.
Et ne nos in- du- cas in ten- ta- ti- o- nem, in ten- ta- ti- o- nem: sed
stris. Et ne nos in- du- cas in ten- ta- ti- o- nem:
ri- bus no- stris. Et ne nos in- du- cas in ten- ta- ti- o- nem, in ten- ta- ti- o- nem: sed li-
Et ne nos in- du- cas in ten- ta- ti- o- nem: sed li- be- ra nos
Et ne nos in- du- cas in ten- ta- ti- o- nem, in ten- ta- ti- o- nem: sed li- be- ra
Et ne nos in- du- cas in ten- ta- ti- o- nem, in ten- ta- ti- o- nem: sed li- be-

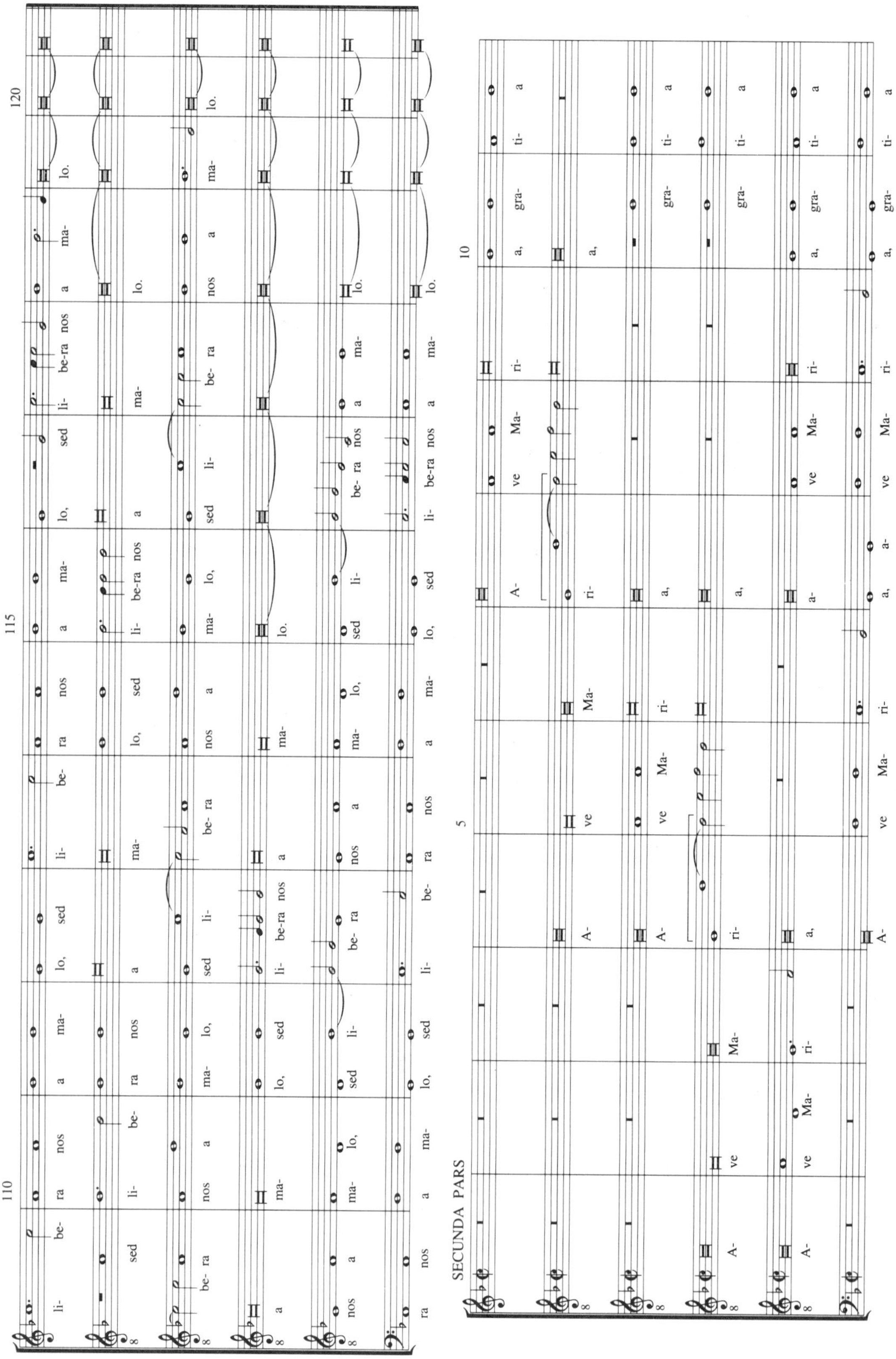

SECUNDA PARS

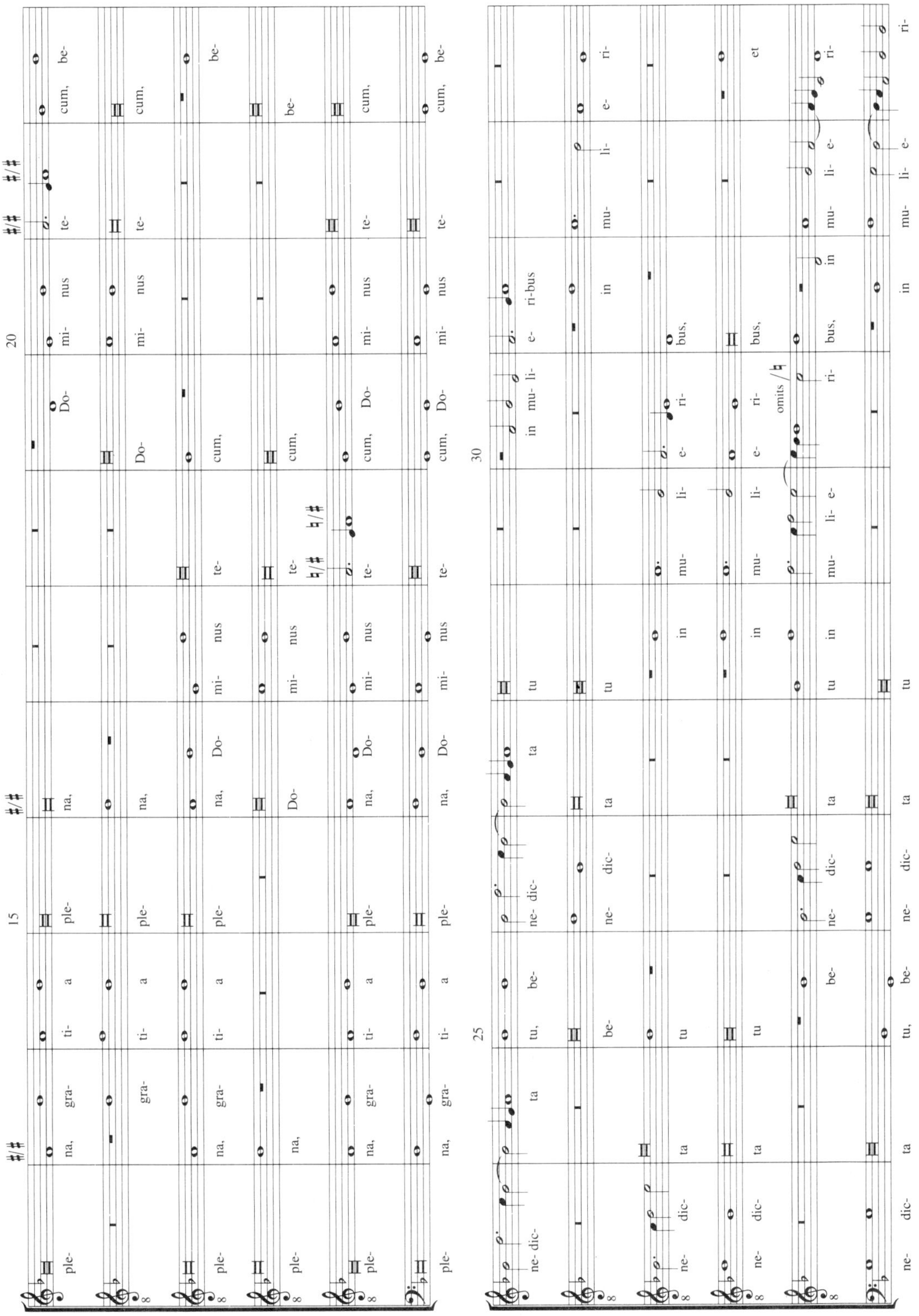
15
20
ple- na, gra- ti- a ple- na, Do- mi- nus te- cum, be-
ple- gra- ti- a ple- na, Do- mi- nus te- cum,
ple- na, gra- ti- a ple- na, Do- mi- nus te- cum, be-
ple- na, Do- mi- nus te- cum, be-
ple- na, gra- ti- a ple- na, Do- mi- nus te- cum, Do- mi- nus te- cum,
ple- na, gra- ti- a ple- na, Do- mi- nus te- cum, Do- mi- nus te- cum, be-
25
30
ne- dic- ta tu, be- ne- dic- ta tu in mu- li- e- ri-bus
ne- dic- ta tu in mu- li- e- ri-
ne- dic- ta tu in mu- li- e- ri- bus,
ne- dic- ta tu in mu- li- e- ri- bus, et
omits ♮
be- ne- dic- ta tu in mu- li- e- ri- bus, in mu- li- e- ri-
ne- dic- ta tu, be- ne- dic- ta tu in mu- li- e- ri-

et be-ne-dic-tus, et be-ne-dic-tus fruc-tus ven-tris tu- i
bus, et be-ne-dic- tus fruc- tus ven-tris
et be-ne- dic- tus, et be-ne- dic- tus fruc- tus ven- tris tu-
be- ne- dic- tus, fruc- tus ven- tris tu- i
bus, et be- ne- dic- tus, et be- ne- dic- tus fruc- tus ven- tris tu- i
bus, et be- ne- dic- tus et be- ne- dic- tus fruc- tus ven- tris
O Je- su Fi- li De- i qui tol- lis pec-
tu- i O Je- su fi- li, fi- li De- i qui
i O Je- su fi- li De- i qui tol- lis
O Je- su fi- li De- i fi- li De- i qui tol- lis pec- ca- ta mun- di
O Je- su fi- li De- i qui tol- lis pec- ca- ta mun- di
tu- i O Je- su fi- li De- i qui

*Gintzler simultaneously employs f♮ and f♯ at this cadence.

Alexander Agricola
'Si Dedero'
Paris, BN 1597,
ff 7v–8r
Superius
Tenor
Contra
Si de- de- ro [si de-
Si de- de- ro
Si dedero somnum
de- ro]
[si de- de- ro]
som-
num o- cu- lis me-
som- num o-
cu- lis [me-
is
is] et pal-
et pal- pe- bris me-
pe- bris [me-
[ms =]

is dor- mi- ta- ti- o- nem [dor- mi- ta- ti- o- nem
is] [dor- mi- ta- ti- o- nem dor- mi- ta- ti- o- nem
dor- mi- ta- ti- o- nem.]
dor- mi- ta- ti- o- nem.]

 # NOTES

Introduction

1 See Tomlinson *Culture* for a discussion of 'thick' and 'thin' contexts as they relate to musicological research.
2 There is at present no reliable way of deducing Josquin's predilections. Josquin wrote, of course, with specific intentions in mind, but these may well be lost to us. We do not know, for example, which theoretical treatises reflect Josquin's thinking on the use of sharps and flats or which vocal sources accurately record his intentions, especially when so many sources were copied or printed after he died. And unfortunately, composers of Josquin's generation, at least according to the theorist Pietro Aaron, could not rely on performers to discover from the notation what Aaron calls the 'intentions and secrets' of the composer (see Chapter 1, 'Theoretical Framework,' for a discussion of the relevant passages from Aaron).

Chapter One

1 Within these broad categories, theorists discuss the addition of sharps and flats in relation to the following topics: (a) the art of counterpoint: discussions of consonance – Bermudo and Ramis; dissonance – Bermudo and Tinctoris; cadences – Zarlino; chromatic genus – Gaffurius; false relations – Zarlino; approaches to perfect intervals – Ornithoparchus; etc; (b) solmization:

discussions of chromaticism – Finck; *fa supra la* – Finck and Ornithoparchus; and cadences – Bourgeois; (c) modes: discussion of cadences – Sancta Maria; and tritones – Tinctoris; (d) *musica ficta*: discussions of hidden semitones – Cochlaeus; and melodic dissonance – Listenius and Ornithoparchus; (e) the semichromatic genus: discussions of chromaticism – Bermudo; (f) the function of sharps and flats: discussions of cadences – Vanneo; black keys – Bermudo; and general uses – Aaron, Lanfranco, and Zarlino.

2 I agree with Howard Brown's conclusion (*Ficta* pp 163–4) that because this issue was a practical and thus extra-theoretical matter, it may never be studied satisfactorily from treatises alone.

3 See, for example, *Dec* IV 48, f 88r, 'vieniendo a unisonus no la [una tercera mayor] haremos cantando, o tañendo,' and *Dec* V 32, f 138v, 'Pues como lo que ahora se tañe, y canta en composicion sea mixto del genero diatonico y chromatico.'

4 *ATF* I 11, f 27v: 'y lo que es incantable no se puede tañer.'

5 Le Roy *Inst* f 6r

6 As early as the late fourteenth century, this understanding existed. In the anonymous Berkeley manuscript, the author stated that the sign for the *coniuncta b mollis* requires the pitch to be lowered by a major semitone and called *fa*; conversely, *b durum* requires the pitch to be raised by a major semitone and called *mi*. Ellsworth *Berkeley* pp 52–3: 'Item ubicumque ponitur signum b debet deprimi sonus verus illius articuli per unum maius semitonum, et dici fa. Et ubi signum ♯ ponitur, sonus illius articuli debet per maius semitonum elevari, et dici ibidem mi.'

7 Ornithoparchus/Dowland *MAM* I 5, pp 21, 136: 'Quoties signatur fa vel mi, preter naturam, oportet solfizantem signaturam sequi, quo ad duraverit.'

8 Similar statements are made in Guilliaud *RMP* I 7, f Aivv and Heyden *AC* I 4, p 24.

9 Ornithoparchus/Dowland *MAM* IV 5, pp 100, 204. Further to the passages cited here, I define primary *clausulae* as those in which the cadence-notes constitute the main structural foundations of the mode. These cadences are derived from the notes bounding the species of fourths and fifths and from the repercussion notes. Secondary cadences can be inserted without disturbing the mode but are not part of the mode's structural foundations. Transitory *clausulae* are formed on cadence-notes foreign to the mode. In addition, my use of the three terms 'subsemitone,' 'subtone,' and 'suprasemitone' may be exemplified by the following cadences:

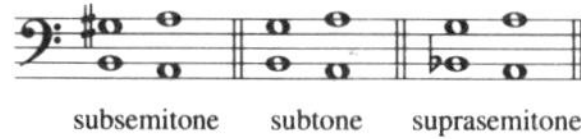

For further discussion of the basic intervallic structure of cadential progressions, see Berger *Musica* pp 122–38.

10 Zarlino *IH* III 53–4, pp 221–6

11 Bourgeois *DCM* pp 60–1

12 Zarlino *IH* III 53, p 223. Although in most *clausulae* cadence-notes are approached by stepwise motion, Zarlino does illustrate progressions in which one of the voices leaps to a perfect consonance:

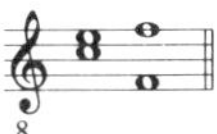

(Zarlino *IH* III 38, p 188).

13 Gaffurius *PM* III 3, f ddiiv; Aaron *IH* III 39, f 50r–v; Ornithoparchus/Dowland *MAM* IV 3, pp 95, 200; Lanfranco *SM* IV, p 116; Vanneo *RMA* III 14, f 75v; and Bermudo *Dec* IV 48, f 87v.

14 According to Bermudo, the subsemitone was incorporated even where its production was exceedingly difficult: 'Dizen, que el nonbrado Ludovico quando venia a clausular: poniendo el dedo debaxo de la cuerda, la semitonava, y hazia clausula de sustentado. Gran destreza y certidumbre era menester para esto'/ 'It is said that the renowned Ludovico [a harpist], when he came to a *clausula*, placed his finger beneath the string, [producing] the semitone, and made a raised cadence. Great skill and accuracy are necessary for this' (Bermudo *Dec* IV 88, f 110v).

15 Bourgeois *DCM* pp 60–1

16 Sancta Maria *ATF* I 24, f 63v

17 In similar melodic lines occurring in *cantus mollis* pieces (that is, pieces with the voice parts prefixed by B♭), the lutenists Melchiore de Barberiis, Diego Pisador, and Sebastian Ochsenkun incorporated both B♭ and F♯. See Josquin Desprez's 'Salve Regina' (69–70, 78–9) and 'Qui habitat' (II 121–2) in Toft *Pitch* vol 2. In these three examples, no *clausula* is formed on the G.

18 I am grateful to Professor Brian Trowell for bringing this passage to my attention. Berger (*Musica* p 102) finds the *Cmi* in bar 3 to be awkward, because the sharp would create the effect of a cadence. I find, however, that the insertion of a sharp at this point is a normal Renaissance procedure which frequently is encountered outside cadential passages. A number of instances of this practice will be discussed in the next chapter.

19 Bermudo *Dec* V 32, ff 138v–39r

20 Aaron *LM* II, ff 8v–9r

21 Bermudo *Dec* V 32, f 139r

22 It should be noted that the intabulations of Josquin's motets do not substantiate these claims.

23 Aaron *Tosc* II 20, f Kv

24 Ramis *MP* pt 1, II 7

25 Zarlino *IH* III 30, pp 180–1

26 This and all those examples from Bermudo given below (Exs 1.14–17) are found in *Dec* V 32. These examples expand on the ones by Pietro Aaron and Luigi Dentice which are cited in Berger *Musica* pp 104, 106.

27 In Ex 1.16, the *tenor*'s B leaps to the E and the *altus* provides the C.

28 For a similar example, see Aaron *LM* II 7, f 7r.

29   Sancta Maria concurs; see Sancta Maria *ATF* I 11, f 27v.

30   Coclico *CM* f Iivv

31   Correa *FO*, Advertencia 17, ff 11v–12v

32   Correa *FO* f 81v: 'en muchos de ellos no ay nota de bequadrado, pero no obsta que la razon la pide, y la fuerça obliga a que la aya'/ 'in many of them [compositions], there is no sign for *bequadrado*. Nevertheless, reason demands it and the force [of the music] requires that it be there.'

33   Cabezón *Obras* f 142r

34   Although Berger (*Musica* pp 99–100) discusses the Tinctoris example, he does not mention Correa or Montanos. I suggest that these two Spanish authors provide the additional theoretical evidence Berger requires in order for him to be convinced of the acceptability of dissonant octaves. Tinctoris probably was not overstating the case with this example (1.20); more than likely, he simply was reporting this aspect of contemporary practice. Our twentieth-century ears may not be the best judge of attitudes toward dissonance in Renaissance society.

35   The E♭ in the *secundus bassus* is notated in a number of sources, but no source seen by me specifies a flat for the *altus* E in bar 67. Furthermore, each of the three intabulators maintains the nonharmonic relations. See Benthem *Fortuna* for further examples of these relations in Josquin's works.

36   Similar conclusions have been drawn in Haar *False*, Benthem *Fortuna*, and Noblitt *Chromatic*. I do not support Berger's notion (*Musica* p 111) that we may infer from Zarlino's discussion of nonharmonic relations that octave cross-relations were more offensive to Renaissance musicians than false relations involving other intervals. Perhaps using our twentieth-century ears as the arbiters of taste for Renaissance society may lead to interpretations which are culturally invalid (see n34, above). I believe, as suggested in Tomlinson *Culture* p 352, that we should establish a 'thick' context for our observations, and at the very least we should take into consideration all of the musical sources, including tablatures.

37   Ornithoparchus/Dowland *MAM* I 10, pp 32, 145 and 7, pp 26, 140

38   Tinctoris *NPT* 8, p 74: 'Notandum autem quod non solum in hiis duobus tonis tritonus est evitandus, sed etiam in omnibus aliis'/ 'Note, however, that the tritone is to be avoided not only in these two modes [five and six] but also in all others.'

39   Listenius *Musica* I 6, f b4v: 'Exempla sunt ubicumque obvia, quare tantum hic exemplum unius vocis.'

40   Aaron *ToscA* f Niir

41   Zarlino *IH* III 57, p 236

42   Praetorius *SM* III 3, p 32

43   Tinctoris *NPT* 8, p 75. He maintained that while it was possible for a singer to use a tritone in a stepwise progression, the tritone leap was either difficult or impossible (*NPT* 8, p 76).

44   Bermudo *Dec* IV 47, f 87r–v
45   Bermudo *Dec* V 32, f 139r–v
46   Sancta Maria *ATF* I 11, ff 28r–29r
47   Glarean *Dod* I 8, p 20
48   Agricola *MCD* 4, f Bvr: 'Wenn aber ein gesang nür durch eine secundam uber das la steiget / und fellet bald widderümb herab ins f faut / so singt man stets fa auff der selbigen noten / Es sey denn das etwa dieser zeichen eins / ♮♯ welche nu bedeuten / im figural gesang sonderlich / bey der selbigen noten erfunden werde'/ 'But when a song ascends only a second above *la* and soon falls back down to F*faut*, then one always sings *fa* on these notes, unless, especially in figural song, one finds these signs ♮ ♯ , which signify *mi*, beside the notes'; Finck *MP* I, f Fr: 'Propter unam notam ascendentem super la, non fit mutatio, sed semper fa in ea est cantandum, nisi hoc ♮ , vel hoc ♯ assignatum sit' / 'When ascending one note above *la*, make no mutation but always sing *fa* in this, unless this ♮ or this ♯ is marked.'
49   Aaron *LM* I 8; Marchettus *Luc* XI 4, pp 398–401
50   Zarlino *IH* III 51, 52, pp 212–20; this concept is elaborated in Haar *Zarlino*. The rhetorical connotations of Renaissance *fugae* are discussed in Butler *Fugue* pp 49–62.

Chapter Two

1   See Lockwood *Dispute*.
2   On Francesco, see Ness *Francesco* p 3; on Cantelmo, see Pope *Vihuela* p 375 n21; on Matelart, see *New Grove* 11: 818; on Narvaez, see Anglés *Música* pp 104–5, 109, 113; and on lutenists in Mantua, see Prizer *Lutenists*.
3   In Amos *Lute*, the following lutenists are listed as singers: Nikolaus Balamanuto (at the court of Innsbruck 1564–80), Tiberius Balamanuto (at the Tirolian court 1582–93), Julio Crema (at the court of Innsbruck 1581–5), Hans von Metz (Kapellmeister ca 1540 at the Hofkapelle in Stuttgart), Johann Stobäus (at the ducal chapel of Konigsberg in 1601, and Kantor of the cathedral of Konigsberg in 1602), Giovanni Vuolpa (at the court of Innsbruck in 1582), and Christoph Westermeier (at the court of Hechingen in 1577).
4   Janssen (*Waytes*, Appendix 2) lists the following Waytes as choristers in the cathedral: Richard Graves (1584–5), Arthur Jackson (1590–1609), Peter Sandlyn (1607), Peter Spratt, Sr (1574–5), and Anthony Wilson (1574–5).
5   Sancta Maria *ATF* I 21, f 57v: 'es cantar cada boz por si, entendiendola Solfa de rayz.'
6   Pisador *LM* ff 17r–24r
7   Milán *EM*, Fuenllana *OL*, Sancta Maria *ATF*, Virdung *MG*, Judenkünig *ASKU*, and

the *Board Lute Book* f [iv]. In this last book, the chart may be in the hand of John Dowland (see the unpaginated commentary in Robert Spencer's facs ed of the *Board Lute Book*).

8   See Milán *EM*, preface and ff B1v–G2r, J1r–P5r; Fuenllana *OL*, preface and ff 170v–72v; and Adriansen *NPM*, preface.

9   On the necessity of adding sharps that were not specified in the vocal source, Le Roy observed, ' … thei doe not use to marke them, in many sortes of songe, savying in this aswell in the Treble, as in other partes' (Le Roy *Inst* f 6r).

10   *New Grove* 5:162

11   See the arguments in Bent *Diatonic* pp 40–4, especially p 44, where Professor Bent recognizes, despite her previous statements, that 'even instrumentalists may have corrected perfect intervals, balanced priorities and matched imitative motives by exercising *the same aural skills as singers*' (emphasis mine). See also the arguments in the *New Grove* 12:807.

12   I am following the concept of hexachords outlined in Ornithoparchus/ Dowland *MAM* I 4, pp 19–20, 134–5; Lanfranco *SM* I, pp 12ff, 26ff; and Cretz *CI* ff B5v–6r (Lanfranco discusses notes of permutation). Furthermore, I agree with Berger's assertion (*Musica* pp 146–7) that one may employ either a sharp or a flat at *clausulae* and that context determines the choice. However, I would augment Berger's statements by suggesting that the role of flats in the sixteenth century was not as limited to the correction of *mi contra fa* as he suspects but frequently included the important function of making the penultimate interval of a cadence a major sixth. Moreover, the table demonstrates that in some German intabulations, cadences on the *repercussio* in the Dorian mode (the note A) more frequently are rendered with a sharp than with a flat. This information seems to contradict Berger's supposition (*Musica* pp 147–8) that a sharped approach to cadences on the *repercussio* would convey a temporary shift to another final.

13   Examples of the latter may be found in motets in *cantus mollis* Dorian, that is, in primary cadences on D ('Praeter rerum' I 48, 50; 'Tribulatio et angustia' 15, 21, 55), and examples of the former in secondary cadences on A ('Ave Maria' 58; 'Qui habitat' I 73, II 40; 'Tribulatio et angustia' 20, 36, 41). Transcriptions of these motets and their printed intabulations appear in Toft *Pitch* vol 2.

14   See Cochlaeus *TM* II 10, f cv and Vanneo *RMA* III 36, f 90r.

15   This may form part of a distinctive German practice, and Chapter 3 will be devoted to a discussion of the German custom. Previously, scholars probably were unaware that such a custom may have existed, and this forced them to search for alternative reasons to explain the absence of subsemitones at cadences. See, for example, Brown *Accidentals* p 483, where Professor Brown suggests that Hans Gerle and Sebastian Ochsenkun did not incorporate the subsemitone at one cadence in order to avoid the chromatic line E♭–D–C♯ –D.

16 I agree with Berger's speculation (*Musica* p 153) that a doubled seventh step at a cadence discouraged the employment of a sharp. But his suggestion that a flattened second step would have been the normal alternative is not supported by tablatures; this was, it seems, only one of the options open to performers (see below).

17 Tinctoris *AC* II 34. See Chapter 1 for the complete quotation. The emphasis is mine.

18 See Berger *Musica* p 152.

19 See also 'Salve regina' 9, 12–14, and 21–2.

20 Interestingly, the passage in 'Benedicta es' is repeated in bars 8–9 and 11–12. Miguel de Fuenllana, however, interprets the passage chromatically on only two of its appearances.

21 As Berger predicted (*Musica* p 150), practical sources do indeed confirm the necessity for a flexible treatment of *clausulae* on the *repercussio*, especially when various notes in the penultimate sonority are doubled. Furthermore, Brown (*Ficta* p 170) cites several instances in the French chanson repertoire from the middle of the sixteenth century where the intabulator Albert de Rippe employed the suprasemitone and the subsemitone simultaneously at cadences on the *repercussio* D in *cantus mollis* Dorian.

22 I am following Howard Brown's nomenclature (*Ficta* pp 172–3) but do not wish to imply a tonal progression by these numbers. Instead, I am using them to designate specific steps in the modal octave.

23 I disagree with Brown's contention (*Ficta* pp 172–3) that lutenists generally were consistent in treating these types of cadences in 'minor' (Brown's term) modes, for the intabulations of Josquin's motets do not support the strength of his conclusion.

24 See Chapter 1 for a discussion of these statements. See also Berger *Musica* pp 138–9.

25 Brown (*Accidentals* p 516) discusses this passage and finds Milano's and Gintzler's treatment of the passage surprising. I suggest, however, that these two performers simply were aligning themselves with those theorists who advocated raising the third at cadences. In fact, these intabulations support Brown's contention (*Accidentals* p 477) that musicians in the sixteenth century were not interested in preserving the purity of the modes. I would take Brown's observation one step further, speculating that in the middle of the sixteenth century the use of sharps and flats, as described in this book, and the concept of mode may well have been interdependent. Lanfranco (*SM* IV, pp 126–7), for example, states that in the scale of *b durum* one uses the *diesis* on the notes C, F, and G and in *b mollis* on C, F, and B♭. This sign, he maintains, is employed to avoid the tritone, to form smoother consonances (the approach to perfect intervals and the raised third at cadences), and to create the subsemitone at cadences where it does not occur naturally. In other words, he implies that sharps will occur frequently in modal polyphony. Thus, we may

have to adjust our modern notion of modal purity if we are willing to accept the idea of sharps' and flats' actually creating the sense of mode for sixteenth-century musicians rather than violating it. For further discussion of modal purity, see the sections of Chapter 4 ('Traditions of Pitch-Content') devoted to Josquin's 'Pater noster' and Agricola's 'Si dedero.'

26   See Chapter 1 for a discussion of these statements. I disagree with Brown's assertion (*Ficta* p 175) that no satisfactory principle can be devised to explain these types of passages. The examples he presents (pp 180, 182) may well be clear instances of the lutenists Albert de Rippe's and Adrian Le Roy's applying this convention to the chanson repertoire.

27   See Chapter 1 for a discussion of Bermudo's comments. The passages given in Example 2.40 also support the following statement in Berger *Musica* p 149: 'We may have here an indication that sixteenth-century musicians could disagree on whether to treat a progression like a cadence or not.'

28   I agree with Berger's assertion (*Musica* pp 118, 147) that from the 1470s flats were used to correct *mi contra fa*, and I might add that they were used frequently. But as intabulations demonstrate, sharps played an important role as well. Perhaps sixteenth-century musicians continued, at least in part, what Berger identifies as an older tradition that existed before the 1470s in which both flats and sharps were used to remove *mi contra fa* (*Musica* p 118). See below for a discussion of an excerpt containing a sharp to eliminate vertical dissonance.

29   A similar passage in Dominique Phinot's motet 'Pater peccavi' presents the performer with the intriguing problem of deciding how to remove the melodic tritone in the *cantus*. If one acknowledges that a number of perform-

Phinot 'Pater peccavi' II 17–21
Source: *Primus liber cum quinque vocibus. Mottetti del frutto.* Venice 1538[4]

ers in the sixteenth century would have felt the strong subsemitonal pull to the structural foundation G, then adopting F♯ in the *cantus* and in the *tenor* not only removes the tritone but also keeps the modern performer well within the bounds of normal Renaissance procedure. The flatward chain-reaction which could be caused by the introduction of B♭ (the flats for this reading are given in square brackets) seems to be outside the intabulators' practices (see the discussion of nonharmonic relations below). I wish to thank Art Levine for bringing this passage to my attention.

30 See Chapter 1 for a discussion of this dilemma.

31 Berger *Musica* pp 70–1, 82

32 Brown (*Accidentals* p 487) discusses the passage from 'Benedicta es,' stating that adding a sharp to only the *tenor*'s F in bar 84 is the correct solution. I submit, however, that no single solution is correct; indeed, a range of acceptable readings appears to have existed for these problematic passages.

33 See Chapter 1 for a discussion of Zarlino's comments.

34 Bermudo *Dec* v 32, f 139r. Cited in Chapter 1.

35 The intabulations contradict the notion expressed in Berger *Musica* p 111 that musicians in the Renaissance tended to avoid cross-relations involving dissonant octaves (and/or unisons). Moreover, passages such as those shown in Examples 2.43 to 2.45 argue against the existence of an unwritten rule known today as 'unity of phrase.' Edward Lowinsky (*Musica Nova* p ix) defines this rule as follows: 'Even the principle of the unity of phrase, which means that frequently a certain accidental exercises its efficacy for the duration of a musical phrase, is fairly well expressed in the prohibition against false relations.' However, the retention of nonharmonic relations was the norm in the sixteenth century, for the removal of false relations is encountered only rarely in the intabulations. Brown (*Accidentals* p 486 Ex 8) cites a passage from 'Qui habitat' (ɪ 101–5) which is supposed to exemplify the unwritten rule of 'unity of phrase,' but unfortunately the passage is not without its problems. The removal of the nonharmonic relation by one of the intabulators, Hans Gerle, created *mi contra fa* vertically. The other two intabulators, Sebastian Ochsenkun and Valentin Bakfark, followed the more common sixteenth-century procedure and simply incurred the false relation. The passage, then, does not demonstrate in a very convincing fashion that such an unwritten rule existed.

36 Blackburn *Lupi* vol 1, pp xxxvi, 144. I disagree with Blackburn's assumption that the dissonance presented in this passage, and elsewhere in the piece, is evidence that Gintzler was asleep while intabulating. The body of evidence which I have presented in this book suggests that Gintzler's practice is truly within the bounds of sixteenth-century style.

37 For other corroborating studies, see Noblitt *Chromatic* pp 35–7; Slim *Versions* pp 143–4; Apel *Punto*; Brown *Ficta* pp 167, 178; and Dahlhaus *Josquin* p 211. See also Hanen *Escorial* vol 1, p 133 and vol 2, pp 199–204 for a piece by

Pullois which contains a notated C♯ against C. All of the examples presented in these studies contradict Berger's view (*Musica* p 100) that vertical imperfect octaves were not allowed in the Renaissance. Apart from the test of his own ears, the only evidence Berger provides to support his statement is information on melodic dissonance, which may not be relevant because we are discussing dissonance between parts, not within a single part. Both theoretical and practical sources confirm the use of dissonant simultaneous octaves during the sixteenth century.

38   Furthermore, one frequently encounters these clashes in purely instrumental genres. See, for example, the *fantaisies* by Albert de Rippe in Vaccaro *Rippe*, especially numbers III (138) and IV (33, 71, 117–18, 347).

39   These passages argue against Berger's statement (*Musica* p 80) that in both transposed and untransposed systems one always corrects the dissonance with the flat and not the sharp, because they show that one of the exceptions to this rule (Berger cites Lanfranco's [1533] endorsing the use of the *diesis* for tempering the tritone [*Musica* p 81]) may be more common than previously considered. Once again, practical sources remind us of how important it is to establish a 'thick' context for the discussion.

Chapter Three

1   Please note that for all of the *clausulae* in which subsemitones occur naturally, for example cadences on the note F, Gerle retains the semitonal motion. He never specifies subtones in these passages. Therefore, the pieces which are classified here as containing only subtonal *clausulae* may in fact include the occasional subsemitonal cadence.

2   See, for example, Blackburn *Lupi* vol 1, p xxxv and Brown *Accidentals* pp 479, 482, 484–5, 490.

Chapter Four

1   The vocal sources for this motet are (a) the following manuscripts: Barcelona, Biblioteca Central, 681; Florence, Biblioteca Medicea-Laurenziana, Acquisti e doni 666; London, British Library, Add 19583; Modena, Duomo, Biblioteca e Archivio Capitolare, Mus IX; Munich, Universitätsbibliothek, 8° 326; Regensburg, Bischöfliche Zentralbibliothek, AR 891–2 and C 120; Saint Gall, Stiftsbibliothek, 463; Seville, Catedral Metropolitana, Bibliteca del Coro, 1; Toledo, Biblioteca Capitular de la Catedral Metropolitana, B.10; Rome,

Biblioteca Apostolica Vaticana, Cappella Sistina 24; and (b) the following printed anthologies: *Motetti de la corona, libro quarto* (Venice 1519[3]); *Liber selectarum cantionum* (Augsburg 1520[4]); *Motetti libro primo* (Venice 1521[3]); [*Motetti et carmina gallica* (Rome ca 1521[7])]; *Secundus tomus novi operis musici* (Nürnberg 1538[3]); *Moduli ex sacris … liber primus* (Paris 1555); *Secunda pars magni operis musici* (Nürnberg 1559[1]); the only sources relevant to this study are those which contain all five vocal parts. The printed intabulations are Hans Gerle, *Tabulatur auff die Laudten* (Nürnberg 1533[1]); Enriquez de Valderrávano, *Silva de sirenas* (Valladolid 1547[5]); Sebastian Ochsenkun, *Tabulaturbuch auff die Lauten* (Heidelberg 1558[5]); Antonio de Cabezón, *Obras de música* (Madrid 1578[3]); for transcriptions of these intabulations see Toft *Pitch* vol 2, pp 99–118.

2 In bar 48 of the *superius*, Ochsenkun employs B♮ .

3 The vocal sources for this motet are (a) the following manuscripts: Brussels, Bibliothèque du Conservatoire Royal de Musique, 27088; Copenhagen, Det Kongelige Bibliothek, Gamle kongelige Samling 1873, 4°; Kassel, Murhard'sche Bibliothek der Stadt Kassel und Landesbibliothek, 4° Mus. 91/1–5; Leipzig, Universitätsbibliothek, Thomaskirche 49 (1–4); and (b) the following printed anthologies: *Liber secundus cantionum sacrarum* (Louvain 1554[2]); *Tertius liber modulorum* (Geneva 1555[13]); *Novum et insigne opus musicum* (Nürnberg 1558[4]). The printed intabulations are Johannes Rühling, *Tabulaturbuch auff Orgeln und Instrument* (Leipzig 1583[6]); Jakob Paix, *Thesaurus motetarum* (Strasburg 1589[6]).

4 For four other discussions of this motet, see Lowinsky *Secret* pp 16–26 and its subsequent defence in Lowinsky *Re-examined* pp 104–7; Elders *Studien* pp 173–82; Beebe *Mode* pp 340–5; and Bentham *Absalon*. None of these authors suggests that varying performing traditions may be associated with the passage in question, nor do they discuss the extant intabulations of the motet.

5 Lowinsky *Secret* pp 16–26. No intabulations support Lowinsky's theories, and his work remains as controversial today as it was forty years ago. My objection to Lowinsky's theory of secret chromaticism centres on his speculative argumentation. He cites no documentary evidence to substantiate his claim that an ostinato (his term) must be solmized in the same way on each recurrence and that a code-note exists. I have provided documentary evidence in this book which contradicts his rigid interpretation of ostinato-like figures, and I maintain that Lowinsky's notion of a code-note does not take into account the flexible practices surrounding the sixteenth-century treatment of dissonance, especially false relations. More specifically, the fundamental problem with Lowinsky's reading of 'Fremuit spiritu Jesus' is that his interpretation is valid only for one source (Brussels 27088); all other surviving vocal sources do not support the idea of chain reaction. Unfortunately, the theory does not find support in tablatures either. Secret chromaticism just does not seem to have been part of the musical vocabulary of intabulators (see

the discussion of 'Absalon, fili mi' below), not even for lutenists where the existence of fret placement approximating equal temperament (see Lindley *Temperaments*, chap 3) made secret chromaticism a very real possibility. For five other recent discussions of secret chromaticism, see Berger *Musica* vol 2, passim; Beebe *Mode*; Benthem *Fortuna* and *Absalon*; and Bent *Diatonic*.

6   Benthem (*Absalon*) argues that 'Absalon, fili mi' may have been composed by Pierre de la Rue rather than Josquin. His arguments, although not conclusive, are persuasive enough that Josquin's authorship now may be questioned legitimately. The identity of the composer, however, does not affect my discussion of the work.

7   Throughout this section the vocal sources will be referred to as Royal 8, 1540^7, and 1559^2. The most striking differences between the printed editions of 'Absalon' and the British Library's manuscript version are a pitch level a ninth lower in Royal 8 and the utilization of differing signatures in this manuscript.

8   1559^2 clearly indicates textual repetition and spreads the notes of each part over a greater number of staves, allowing more room to place the text under the appropriate notes.

9   See bars 10–16, 60–5, and 77–82. Short examples will be included within the main body of the text. Please refer to the Appendix for the lengthier passages.

10 That E♭ regularly was included in pieces in *cantus mollis* Lydian at least by the 1530s can be gleaned from vihuela instruction-books which designate the mode of each piece. See, for example, Fantasia 19 and Pavana 3 in Luis Milán's *El Maestro*, in Jacobs *Milán* pp 82–7, 104–5.

11 For a general introduction to the influences of rhetorical thought on music, see Bartel *Handbuch*, Buelow *Rhetoric*, Palisca *Rhetorical*, and Unger *Rhetoric*.

12 Normal procedure from the middle of the sixteenth century includes the employment of subsemitones at all cadence points and the use of E♭ to correct *mi contra fa*. In practice, these two factors cause an increase in the number of oscillatory areas within the mode. This increase results in frequent *mi-fa* clashes between E♮ and E♭, B♮ and B♭, and, if the transitory cadence-note G is present, F♯ and F♮. For unmistakable examples of these procedures, see the following mode five and six pieces in vihuela tablatures: Milán, *El Maestro*, Fantasia 19, in Jacobs *Milán* pp 82–7 and Fuenllana, *Orphenica lyra*, Fantasias 33–6 and Tiento in Tone VI, in Jacobs *Fuenllana* pp 526–40, 983–4.

13 For an analysis of the latter parts of these sections in modern tonal terms, see Novack *Tonal*. However, since the necessary terminology and techniques for analyzing sixteenth-century music were developed in the early 1600s, I believe that contemporary and near-contemporary tools yield a more accurate understanding of compositional processes.

14 See bars 52–60.

15 See bars 60–8.

16 Johannes Nucius in his *Musices poeticae* ([Neisse 1613] f A4r) identified Josquin

as one of the new rhetorically expressive composers. Burmeister (*Musica poetica* pp 63–4) defines *climax* as the stepwise repetition of a melodic fragment. A discussion of Burmeister's figures and their application in Lasso's motet 'In me transierunt' appears in Palisca *Rhetorical*.

17 In rhetoric, *climax* is a ladder form in which a repeated word links the preceding step to the following (see Sonnino *Handbook* pp 101–2). The composer, too, links his steps, as the last note of one fragment becomes the first of the next. See, for example, bars 61–5 of the *bassus*.

18 The term 'modulation' has been used to describe this and other similar procedures. See Lowinsky *Re-examined*, where Professor Lowinsky reviews his theories on modulatory techniques in sixteenth-century music. But the anachronistic discussion of Renaissance music can be misleading. See Benthem *Fortuna*, in which Benthem discusses Lowinsky's theories on Josquin's 'Fortuna dun gran tempo' and presents a fresh view of this piece. However, three other contemporary interpretations of pitch-content in 'Fortuna' exist that are yet again different from the Spinacino intabulation examined by both Benthem and Lowinsky. See Berlin, Staatsbibliothek, ms 40026 (Leonard Kleber tablature) ff 20–21, in Warburton *Josquin* pp 95–6; and Basel, Universitätsbibliothek, ms F.VI.26(C) (Fundamentum for Oswald Holzach) ff 7v–8v and ms F.IX.22 (Johannes Kotter tablature) ff 18–19v, in Marx *Tabulaturen* pp 95–6, 16–17.

19 See the *Census-Catalogue* vol 2, pp 103–4 for a listing of the most important literature pertaining to this manuscript and for a summary of the views on its dating and provenance; see also Benfield *Royal*.

20 He also employs the rhythmic variants of the printed version in bar 15 of the *contratenor* and bar 41 of the *bassus*, but in both these cases, longer notes are divided into shorter values – a practice commonly employed by Ochsenkun and other lutenists when intabulating semibreves. See bars 1, 4, 6, 8, etc, in the 'Absalon' intabulation (Toft *Pitch* vol 2) and the statement by Adrian Le Roy in his *A Briefe and plaine Instruction*, f 4: 'But in the other two instruments [lutes and virginals] their sound, which dependeth altogither by the toutch of the fingers, cannot endure longer then a semibreve … which is the reason in consequence, that forceth us when we set in Tablature, to devide Maxims always in eight partes, Longes in foure, Breves in two, and so forth of other great notes which are augmented with pricks.'

21 See above for a discussion of the solmization of this passage.

22 Further examples of nonharmonic relations occur in bars 41–2 and in bar 51 (Toft *Pitch* vol 2).

23 See, for instance, Ex 4.12, bar 56. At times, the subsemitone is included in an anticipatory ornamental figure that causes momentary direct dissonance with a lower voice. See bars 25 and 33 (Toft *Pitch* vol 2).

24 B♮ is found in the following bars: 2–3, 11, 19–20, 22, 35, 37–8, 41, 55, 59–60, 67–8, 72, 76–7, and 84 (Toft *Pitch* vol 2).

25 Francesco omits the penultimate note C in three cadences on D (II 31, 62, 65). The Appendix contains an edition of this motet; please refer to it for all music examples.

26 Lanfranco *SM* pp 126–7

27 There is, however, little divergence between the two musicians in cadences on G.

28 Copenhagen, Det Kongelige Bibliotek, Gamle kongelige Samling 1872, 4°; Dresden, Sachsische Landesbibliothek, Glashütte 5 (1–2); Leipzig, Universitätsbibliothek, Thomaskirche 49 (1–4); Munich, Bayerische Staatsbibliothek, Musiksammlung, 12; Padua, Biblioteca Capitolare, A17; Rome, Biblioteca Vallicelliana, s$^\text{I}$ 35–40; Toledo, Biblioteca Capitular de la Catedral Metropolitana, B.18; *Novum et insigne opus musicum* (Nürnberg 1537[1]); *Novum et insigne opus musicum* (Nürnberg 1558[4]).

29 The mensural sources for this motet are (a) the following manuscripts: Barcelona, Biblioteca Central, 454; Bologna, Civico Museo Bibliografico Musicale, Q16, Q17, and Q18; Brussels, Bibliothèque Royale, 11239; Copenhagen, Det Kongelige Bibliotek, Ny kongelige Samling 1848, 2°; Florence, Duomo, Archivio Musicale dell'Opera di Santa Maria del Fiore, 27; Florence, Biblioteca Nazionale Centrale, Magliabechi XIX.178 and Banco Rari 229; Florence, Biblioteca Riccardiana, 2356 and 2794; Greifswald, Universitätsbibliothek, BW 640–1; Munich, Bayerische Staatsbibliothek, Musiksammlung, 3154; Paris, Bibliothèque Nationale, Département de la Musique, Fonds du Conservatoire, Rés Vm^7 676; Paris Bibliothèque Nationale, Département des Manuscrits, Fonds Français, 1597; Rome, Biblioteca Casanatense, 2856; Saint Gall, Stiftsbibliothek, 462 and 463; Segovia, Archivo Capitular de la Catedral, s.s.; Vatican City, Biblioteca Apostolica Vaticana, Cappella Giulia XIII, 27; Verona, Biblioteca Capitolare, DCCLVII; and (b) the following printed anthologies: *Harmonice musices Odhecaton A* (Venice 1501); *Trium vocum carmina a diversi musicis composta* (Nürnberg 1538[9]). The tablature sources are (a) the following keyboard anthologies: Johannes Kotter (Basel, Universitätsbibliothek, F.IX.22); Fridolin Sicher (Saint Gall, Stiftsbibliothek, Cod 530); and (b) the following lute anthologies: Francesco Spinacino, *Intabulatura de Lauto, Libro secondo* (Venice 1507[1]); Vincenzo Capirola (Chicago, Newberry Library, 107501); Hans Newsidler, *Der ander Theil des Lautenbuchs* (Nürnberg 1536[7]). One of these sources, Saint Gall 463, labels the motet as a 'Hypomixolydius' piece. On changing *tetrardus* mode into transposed *protus*, the theorist Ornithoparchus (1517) states, 'Cantus in Gsolreut termi[n]atus: signato fa in bfa♮ mi, est primi vel secundi toni ad quartam transpositi'/ 'A Song ending in *Gsolreut*, marking *fa* in *bfa♮ mi* is of the first or second *Tone* transposed to the fourth' (Ornithoparchus/Dowland *MAM* I 11, pp 35, 148).

30 I will limit my discussion to the three main signature traditions associated with the motet. Although only the *superius* part of Saint Gall 463 survives, I

have included it in the list of hypomixolydian sources because of the rubric in the manuscript, which places the motet in this mode. Greifswald 640–1 also may belong to this group of sources, for both the *superius* and *contra* are in the scale of *b durum*; unfortunately, the *tenor* part is missing, preventing me from confirming this hypothesis. Barcelona 454 (♮ ♮ E♭), Florence 2356 (♭ ♮ ♮), and Florence 2794 (♭♭ ♮) lie outside the main signature traditions of the work.

31 Curiously, Brussels 11239 also incorporates an E♭ in bar 50 of the *contra*. This flat not only introduces a linear tritone into the *contra* part but also creates vertical dissonance with the B above. Perhaps the *tenor*'s B should be rendered as a B♭; however, no documentary evidence exists to support this hypothesis. Two other flat signs are marked in the hypomixolydian sources (Florence 229: *tenor*, B♭ in bar 52; and Saint Gall 462 and 1538[9]: *contra*, B♭ in bar 54). In both cases, the flats remind singers to avoid linear tritones.

32 An edition of 'Si dedero' appears in the Appendix; please refer to it for the lengthier passages.

33 Capirola omits the E in bar 34 of the *contra* and renders the one in bar 35 as E♮.

34 See Chapter 1 for a discussion of the relevant statements.

35 See *superius*, 34, 52, 66–8, 73, and 75; *tenor*, 31, 33, 51, and 71; and *contra*, 19, 36, 67, 68, and 70.

Conclusion

1 Modern performers may even wish to reproduce in their own performances certain aspects of the sixteenth-century instrumentalist's style of ornamentation. Intabulators often changed the melodic structure of a piece by superimposing ornamental figuration on individual voice-parts in such a way that it became possible for them to incorporate sharps and flats on notes that did not exist in the vocal model (see Exs 2.21, 2.35, 2.48, 2.49, 2.51, 2.60, 2.62, 4.12 [bar 22], 4.13), and singers of the time might have employed similar techniques of ornamentation. See Brown *Embellishment* for a discussion of Italian intabulations, especially his Ex 2 on pp 64–5, which, if compared with embellishment manuals from the period, reveals that lutenists used many of the same sorts of figures as singers.

# GLOSSARY

b durum	sharp
b mollis	flat
bequadrado	sharp
b rotondo	flat
cadenza	cadence
clausula	cadence
clavis	key, the seven note-identifying letters a-b-c-d-e-f-g
climax	musical-rhetorical term for the stepwise repetition of a melodic fragment
comes	the following voice in a mimetic passage
compás	*tactus*, or the up and down motion of the hand in beating time
concentus	the vertical combination of notes sounding together
coniuncta	making a whole step into a half step or a half step into a whole step by placing *b mollis* or *b durum* in an irregular place, that is, in a place where they normally would not appear
deductio	one particular hexachord in a specific range
diapason	octave
diapason superflua	augmented octave
diapente	perfect fifth
diatesseron	perfect fourth
diesis	sharp
ditone	major third
dux	*guida*, the leading voice in a mimetic passage
epidiapente	the fifth above

fa	refers to the solmization syllable, or may mean flat; for example, B*fa* = B♭
fa supra la	an abbreviation for the Latin phrase 'unicâ notulâ ascendente supra la, semper canendum esse fa' (one note ascending above *la* always is sung as *fa*)
finalis	the final of a mode
fuga	*mimesis* involving the literal repetition of the solmization syllables of the *guida* by the other voices
guida	the leading voice in a mimetic passage
hexachord	a series of six notes carrying the solmization syllables *ut-re-mi-fa-sol-la* and always containing the interval relationship tone-tone-semitone-tone-tone between the notes; in the scales of *b durum* (pieces with no signature) and *b mollis* (pieces with B♭ in the signature), hexachords are built on the notes G, C, and F and are labelled respectively hard, natural, and soft; hexachords may be constructed on other notes, in which case they are called fictive (because these hexachords lie outside the normal system)
hypotyposis	generic term used by *musica poetica* theorists to designate compositional techniques that function to illustrate words and ideas in a text
imitatione	*mimesis* in which the solmization syllables of the *guida* are modified when they are repeated by the other voices; for example, the interval of a major third in the *guida* (solmized *ut-mi*) may become a minor third in the *comes* (solmized *re-fa*)
imperfect sixth	minor sixth
imperfect third	minor third
kreutzlein	sharp
mi	refers to the solmization syllable, or may mean sharp; for example, C*mi* = C♯
mi contra fa	*mi* against *fa*, the simultaneous sounding of *mi* in one voice and *fa* in another; this produces dissonant relationships, the most common being B (*mi*) against F (*fa*) and E (*mi*) against B♭ (*fa*)
mimesis	generic term for all imitative compositional techniques
mutation	the changing of one solmization syllable into another in order to sing a melody whose range extends beyond a single hexachord
nonharmonic relation	false relation, non-simultaneous
octava mayor	augmented octave

perfect sixth	major sixth
perfect third	major third
pitch-content	the pitches to be performed in a piece of music
punto intenso contra remisso	an intense (sharped) note sounding against a relaxed (lowered) note; this produces dissonant octaves and unisons, for example, C against C♯
remisso	relaxed or lowered
repercussio	the reciting note of a mode; in Dorian on D this note is A, but in Hypodorian on D it is F
semidiapason	diminished octave
semidiapente	diminished fifth
semiditone	minor third
solfa	solmization
solmization	a method of sight-singing using hexachords to establish the interval relationships between notes; for example, to sing a perfect fourth one could employ, depending on the context, the syllables *ut-fa*, *re-sol*, or *mi-la*
sostenido	sharped
subintellectum	understood; for example, the phrase *semitonium subintellectum* may be translated as 'understood semitone,' that is, a semitone which is not notated but should be sung
subsemitone	the semitone below
subtone	the whole tone below
suprasemitone	the semitone above
supratone	the whole tone above
tonus	whole tone
tritonus	tritone
voces	the hexachord syllables *ut-re-mi-fa-sol-la*

BIBLIOGRAPHY

Theoretical Treatises

Aaron *ToscA* — Aaron, Pietro. *Aggiunta (Toscanello in musica)*. Venice 1529; facs Bologna 1969

Aaron *IH* — — *Libri tres de institutione harmonica*. Bologna 1516; facs New York 1976

Aaron *LM* — — *Lucidario in Musica*. Venice 1545; facs New York 1978

Aaron *Tosc* — — *Toscanello in musica*. Venice 1529; facs Bologna 1969

Adriansen *NPM* — Adriansen, Emanuel. *Novum Pratum Musicum*. Antwerp 1592

Agricola *MCD* — Agricola, Martin. *Musica choralis deudsch*. Wittenberg 1533; facs Hildesheim 1969

Artusi *L'Artusi* — Artusi, Giovanni Maria. *L'Artusi ouero delle imperfettioni della moderna musica*. Venice 1600; facs Bologna 1968

Bermudo *Dec* — Bermudo, Juan. *Declaración de instrumentos musicales*. Osuna 1555; facs Kassel 1957

Blahoslav *Musica* — Blahoslav, Jan. *Musica*. Olomouc 1558. In Sovik *Theorists*

Bourgeois *DCM* — Bourgeois, Loys. *Le droict chemin de musique*. Genève 1550; facs Kilkenny 1982

Burmeister *MP* — Burmeister, Joachim. *Musica poetica*. Rostock 1606

Burzio *MO* — Burzio, Nicolo. *Musices opusculum*. Bologna 1487; facs Bologna 1969

Cochlaeus *TM* — Cochlaeus, Johannes. *Tetrachordum musices*. Nürnberg 1512; facs Hildesheim 1971

Coclico *CM*   Coclico, Adrianus Petit. *Compendium musices*. Nürnberg 1552; facs Kassel 1954

Correa *FO*   Correa, Francisco. *Facultad orgánica*. Alcala 1626; facs Geneva 1981

Cretz *CI*   Cretz, Ioannem. *Compendiosa introductio in choralem musicam*. Augsburg 1553

Ellsworth *Berkeley* University of California, Berkeley, Music Library, ms 744. In Ellsworth *Berkeley*

Finck *PM*   Finck, Hermann. *Practica musica*. Wittenberg 1556; facs Bologna 1969

Fuenllana *OL*   Fuenllana, Miguel de. *Orphenica lyra*. Seville 1554; facs Geneva 1981

Gaffurius *PM*   Gaffurius, Franchino. *Practica musice*. Milan 1496; facs New York 1979

Galilei *FD*   Galilei, Vincenzo. *Fronimo Dialogo*. Venice 1568; rev Venice 1584

Gerle *MT*   Gerle, Hans. *Musica und tabulatur*. Nürnberg 1546

Gerle *TL*   — *Tabulatur auff die Laudten*. Nürnberg 1533

Glarean *Dod*   Glarean, Heinrich. *Dodecachordon*. Basel 1547; facs New York 1967

Guilliaud *RMP*   Guilliaud, Maximilian. *Rudiments de musique practique*. Paris 1554; facs Geneva 1981

Hessen *Etlicher*   Hessen, Paul and Bartholomeus. *Etlicher gutter Teutscher und Polnischer Tenz*. Breslau 1555

Hessen *Viel*   — *Viel feiner lieblicher stücklein*. Breslau 1555

Heyden *AC*   Heyden, Sebald. *De arte canendi*. Nürnberg 1540; facs New York 1969

Judenkünig *ASKU*   Judenkünig, Hans. *Ain schone künstliche*. Vienna 1523

Lanfranco *SM*   Lanfranco, Giovanni Maria. *Scintille di musica*. Brescia 1533; facs Bologna 1970

Le Roy *Inst*   Le Roy, Adrian. *A briefe and plaine Instruction to set all Musicke of eight divers tunes in Tableture for the Lute*. London 1574

Listenius *Musica*   Listenius, Nicolaus. *Musica*. Nürnberg 1549; facs Berlin 1927

Marchettus *Luc*   Marchettus da Padua. *Lucidarium*. Ms ca 1318. In Herlinger

Martínez *ACL*   Martínez de Biscargui, Goncalo. *Arte de canto Llano*. Zaragoza 1538; ed in Seay *Martínez*

Milán *EM*   Milán, Luis. *El maestro*. Valencia 1536; facs Geneva 1975

Montanos *AM*   Montanos, Francisco de. *Arte de música*. Valladolid 1592

Morley *PEI*   Morley, Thomas. *A plaine and easie introduction to practicall musicke*. London 1597; facs Amsterdam 1969

Nucius *MP*   Nucius, Johannes. *Musices poeticae*. Neisse 1613

Ornithoparchus/
  Dowland *MAM*   Ornithoparchus, Andreas. *Musica active micrologus*. Leipzig 1517. Trans John Dowland as *Andreas Ornithoparcus His Micrologus, or Introduction*. London 1609; facs New York 1973

Panhormitano *DQM*   Panhormitano, Bartolomeo Lieto. *Dialogo quarto di musica*. Naples 1559

Pisador *LM*   Pisador, Diego. *Libro de música de vihuela*. Salamanca 1552; facs Geneva 1973

Praetorius *SM*   Praetorius, Michael. *Syntagma musicum*, III. Wolfenbüttel 1619; facs Kassel 1958

Ramis *MP*   Ramis de Pareia, Bartolomeo. *Musica practica*. Bologna 1482; facs Bologna 1969

Sancta Maria *ATF*   Sancta Maria, Tomás de. *Arte de tañer fantasía*. Valladolid 1565; facs Geneva 1973

Tinctoris *AC*   Tinctoris, Johannes. *Liber de arte contrapuncti*. Ms 1477. In Seay *Tinctoris 2*

Tinctoris *NPT*   — *Liber de natura et proprietate tonarum*. Ms 1476. In Seay *Tinctoris 1*

Tovar *LMP*   Tovar, Francisco. *Libro de música prática*. Barcelona 1510

Ugolino *DMD*   Ugolino of Orvieto. *Declaratio musice discipline*. Ms ca 1430. In Hughes *Ficta*

Vanneo *RMA*   Vanneo, Stephano. *Recanetum de musica aurea*. Rome 1533; facs Kassel 1969

Vicentino *AM*   Vicentino, Nicola. *L'antica musica ridotta alla moderna prattica*. Rome 1555; facs Kassel 1959

Virdung *MG*   Virdung, Sebastian. *Musica getutscht*. Strasbourg 1511

Zarlino *IH* III   Zarlino, Gioseffo. *Le istitutioni harmoniche*. Venice 1558; facs New York 1965

Tablature Sources

PRINTS

1507₁   Spinacino, Francesco. *Intabulatura de Lauto, Libro primo*. Venice 1507

1533₁   Gerle, Hans. *Tabulatur auff die Laudten*. Nürnberg 1533

1536₃   Francesco da Milano. *Intabolatura di Liuto*. Venice 1536

1536₇   Newsidler, Hans. *Der ander theil des Lautenbuchs*. Nürnberg 1536

1546₄   Barberiis, Melchior de. *Intabulatura di Lautto, Libro sesto*. Venice 1546

1546₇   Francesco da Milano. *Intabolatura de Lauto, Libro segondo*. Venice 1546

1547₃   Gintzler, Simon. *Intabolatura de Lauto, Libro primo*. Venice 1547

1547₅   Valderrávano, Enriquez de. *Silva de sirenas*. Valladolid 1547

1547₉   Teghi, Pierre di. *Des chansons & Motetz Reduictz en Tabulature de Luc*. Louvain 1547

154?₄   Francesco da Milano. *Intabolatura de Leuto*. np, before 1536

1551₁   Gorlier, Simon. *Le Troysieme Livre ... en tabulature de Guiterne*. Paris 1551

1552₇   Pisador, Diego. *Libro de Música de Vihuela*. Salamanca 1552

1552₁₁   Phalèse, Pierre [publisher]. *Hortus Musarum*. Louvain 1552

1553₃   Braysssing, Gregoire. *Quart Livre de Tabulature de Guiterre*. Paris 1553

1553₁₀   Phalèse, Pierre [publisher]. *Horti Musarum secunda pars*. Louvain 1553

1554₃   Fuenllana, Miguel de. *Orphenica Lyra*. Seville 1554

1555₄   Rippe, Albert de. *Cinquiesme Livre de Tabulature de Leut*. Paris 1555

1556₂   Drusina, Benedikt de. *Tabulatura*. Frankfurt 1556

1556₅₋₆   Heckel, Wolff. *Discant Lautten Buch. Tenor Lautten Buch*. Strasbourg 1556

1558₅   Ochsenkun, Sebastian. *Tabulaturbuch auff die Lauten*. Heidelberg 1558

1558₆   Rippe, Albert de. *Sixiesme Livre de Tabulature de Leut*. Paris 1558

1563₁₂   Phalèse, Pierre [publisher]. *Theatrum Musicum*. Louvain 1563

1565₁   Bakfark, Valentin. *Harmoniarum Musicarum ... Tomus primus*. Krakow 1565

1568₇   Phalèse, Pierre [publisher]. *Luculentum Theatrum Musicum*. Louvain 1568

1569₁   Bakfark, Valentin. *Harmoniarum Musicarum ... Tomus primus*. Antwerp 1569

1571₆   Phalèse, Pierre and Jean Bellère [publishers]. *Theatrum Musicum*. Louvain 1571

1574₅   Newsidler, Melchior. *Teutsch Lautenbuch*. Strasbourg 1574

1578₃   Cabezón, Antonio de. *Obras de Música*. Madrid 1578

1583₆   Rühling, Johannes. *Tabulaturbuch auff Orgeln und Instrument*. Leipzig 1583

1589₆   Paix, Jakob. *Thesaurus motetarum*. Strasbourg 1589

MANUSCRIPTS

Capirola, Vincenzo. Chicago, Newberry Library, 107501

Kotter, Johannes. Basel, Universitätsbibliothek, F.IX.22

Sicher, Fridolin. Saint Gall, Stiftsbibliothek, Cod 530

Secondary Literature

AcM   *Acta musicologica*

AM   *Analecta musicologica*

AnM   *Annales musicologiques*

BAMS   *Bulletin of the American Musicological Society*

CM   *Current Musicology*

CMM   Corpus mensurabilis musicae

CMS	*College Music Symposium*
CSM	Corpus scriptorum de musica
EM	*Early Music*
JAMIS	*Journal of the American Musical Instrument Society*
JAMS	*Journal of the American Musicological Society*
JLSA	*Journal of the Lute Society of America*
JM	*Journal of Musicology*
JMT	*Journal of Music Theory*
LSJ	*Lute Society Journal*
MA	*Music Analysis*
MD	*Musica disciplina*
MF	*Music Forum*
ML	*Music and Letters*
MQ	*Musical Quarterly*
MR	*Music Review*
MSD	Musicological Studies and Documents
NRFH	*Nueva revista de filología hispánica*
PAPS	*Proceedings of the American Philosophical Society*
PRMA	*Proceedings of the Royal Musical Association*
RBM	*Revue belge de musicologie*
RM	*Revue de musicologie*
TVNM	*Tijdschrift van de vereniging voor Nederlandse muziekgeschiedenis*

Aldrich *Approach*	Aldrich, Putnam. 'An Approach to the Analysis of Renaissance Music.' MR 30 (1969) 1–21
Allaire *Theory*	Allaire, Gaston G. *The Theory of Hexachords, Solmization, and the Modal System.* MSD 24. Np 1972
Amos *Lute*	Amos, Charles Nelson. 'Lute Practice and Lutenists in Germany between 1500 and 1750.' PHD diss, University of Iowa 1975
Anglés *Música*	Anglés, Higinio. *La música en la Corte de Carlos V.* Monumentos de la música española, vol 2. Barcelona 1965
Apel *Accidentien*	Apel, Willi. *Accidentien und Tonalität in den Musikdenkmälern des 15. und 16. Jahrhunderts.* Strassburg 1937; repr Baden-Baden 1972
Apel *Partial*	— 'The Partial Signatures in the Sources up to 1450.' *AcM* 10 (1938) 1–13
Apel *Postscript*	— 'A Postscript to "The Partial Signatures in the Sources up to 1400."' *AcM* 11 (1939) 40–2
Apel *Punto*	— 'Punto intenso contra remisso.' In *Music East and West* ed Thomas Noblitt (New York 1981) 175–82

176   *Bibliography*

Atcherson *Modal*   Atcherson, Walter Thomas. 'Modal Theory of Sixteenth-Century German Theorists.' PHD diss, Indiana University 1960

Atcherson *Theory*   — 'Theory Accommodates Practice: *Confinalis* Theory in Renaissance Music Treatises.' *JAMS* 23 (1970) 326–30

Bartel *Handbuch*   Bartel, Dietrich. *Handbuch der musikalischen Figurenlehre.* Laaber 1985

Beebe *Mode*   Beebe, Ellen. 'Mode, Structure, and Text Expression in the Motets of Jacobus Clemens non Papa: A Study of Style in Sacred Music.' PHD diss, Yale University 1976

Benfield *Royal*   Benfield, Judith. 'MS. Royal 8.G.vii of the British Library, London.' MMUS thesis, King's College, University of London 1979

Bent *Diatonic*   Bent, Margaret. 'Diatonic *Ficta.*' *Early Music History* 4 (1984) 1–48

Bent *Musica*   — 'Musica Recta and Musica Ficta.' *MD* 26 (1972) 73–100

Bent *Resfacta*   — '*Resfacta* and *Cantare Super Librum.*' *JAMS* 36 (1983) 371–91

Bent *Criteria*   — 'Some Criteria for Establishing Relationships between Sources of Late-Medieval Polyphony.' In Fenlon *MMEME* pp 295–317

Benthem *Fortuna*   Benthem, Jaap Van. 'Fortuna in Focus.' *TVNM* 30 (1980) 1–50

Benthem *Absalon*   — 'Lazarus versus Absalon: About Fact and Fiction in the Netherlands Motet.' *TVNM* 39 (1989) 54–82

Berger *Common*   Berger, Karol. 'The Common and the Unusual Steps of *Musica Ficta*: A Background for the Gamut of Orlando di Lasso's *Prophetiae Sibyllarum.*' *RBM* 39–40 (1985–6) 61–73

Berger *Expanding*   — 'The Expanding Universe of *Musica Ficta* in Theory from 1300 to 1550.' *JM* 4 (1985–6) 410–30

Berger *Martyrdom*   — 'The Martyrdom of St Sebastian: The Function of Accidental Inflections in Dufay's *O beate Sebastiane.*' *EM* 17 (1989) 342–57

Berger *Musica*   — *Musica Ficta.* Cambridge 1987

Berger *Tonality*   — 'Tonality and Atonality in the Prologue to Orlando di Lasso's *Prophetiae Sibyllarum*: Some Methodological Problems in Analysis of Sixteenth-Century Music.' *MQ* 66 (1980) 484–504

Bergquist *Mode* Bergquist, Peter. 'Mode and Polyphony around 1500: Theory and Practice.' MF 1 (1967) 99–161

Bergquist *Theoretical* — 'The Theoretical Writings of Pietro Aaron.' PHD diss, Columbia University 1964

Bergquist *Aaron* — trans. *Pietro Aaron, Toscanello in Music*. 3 vols. Colorado Springs 1970

Blackburn *Lupi* Blackburn, Bonnie J., ed. *Johannes Lupi, Opera Omnia*. CMM 84. Neuhausen-Stuttgart 1980–

Blackman *Judenkünig* Blackman, Martha. 'A Translation of Hans Judenkünig's *Ain schone künstliche Underweisung … (1523).*' LSJ 14 (1972) 29–41

Boorman *Limitations* Boorman, Stanley. 'Limitations and Extensions of Filiation Technique.' In Fenlon MMEME pp 319–46

Boyd *Structural* Boyd, Malcolm. 'Structural Cadences in the Sixteenth-Century Mass.' MR 33 (1972) 1–13

Bray *Ficta* Bray, Roger. 'The Interpretation of Musica Ficta in English Music c. 1490–c. 1580.' PRMA 97 (1970–1) 29–45

Brook *Perspectives* Brook, Barry S., et al. *Perspectives in Musicology*. New York 1972

Brown *Accidentals* Brown, Howard Mayer. 'Accidentals and Ornamentation in Sixteenth-Century Intabulations of Josquin's Motets.' In Lowinsky *Josquin* pp 475–522

Brown *Embellishment* — 'Embellishment in Early Sixteenth-Century Italian Intabulations.' PRMA 100 (1973–4) 49–83

Brown *Bibliography* — *Instrumental Music Printed before 1600: A Bibliography*. Cambridge, Mass. 1965

Brown *Ficta* — 'La Musica Ficta dans les mises en tablatures d'Albert de Rippe et Adrian Le Roy.' In *Le Luth et sa musique II*, ed Jean-Michel Vaccaro (Paris 1984) 163–82

Brown *Review* Review of *Œuvres d'Albert de Rippe*, vol 3, ed Jean-Michel Vaccaro (Paris 1975). ML 57 (1976) 441–3

Buelow *Rhetoric* Buelow, George J. 'Rhetoric and Music.' *New Grove* 15: 793–803

Butler *Fugue* Butler, Gregory G. 'Fugue and Rhetoric.' JMT 21 (1977) 49–109

Caldwell *Editing* Caldwell, John. *Editing Early Music*. Oxford 1985

Caldwell *Musica* — 'Musica Ficta.' EM 13 (1985) 407–8

Carvel *Ficta* Carvel, Bruce Ray. 'A Practical Guide to *Musica Ficta*: Based on an Analysis of Sharps Found in the Music Prints of Ottaviano Petrucci (1501–1519).' PHD diss, Washington University 1982

Census-Catalogue   *Census-Catalogue of Manuscript Sources of Polyphonic Music 1400–1550*, vols 1–5. Neuhausen-Stuttgart 1979–88

CS   Coussemaker, E. de. *Scriptorum de musica medii aevi*. 4 vols. Paris 1864–76

Crawford *Ficta*   Crawford, David. 'Performance and the Laborde Chansonnier: Authenticity of Multiplicities: Musica Ficta.' CMS 10 (1970) 107–11

Dahlhaus *Josquin*   Dahlhaus, Carl. 'Zur Akzidentiensetzung in den Motetten Josquins des Prez.' In *Musik und Verlag* ed Richard Baum and Wolfgang Rehm (Kassel 1968) 206–19

Daniels *Salinas*   Daniels, Arthur M. 'The De Musica Libri VII of Francisco de Salinas.' PHD diss, University of Southern California 1962

Dill *Articulation*   Dill, Charles W. 'Non-Cadential Articulation of Structure in Some Motets by Josquin and Mouton.' CM 33 (1982) 37–55

Doe *Ficta*   Doe, Paul. 'Another View of Musica Ficta in Tudor Music.' PRMA 98 (1971–2) 113–22

Dombois *Gerle*   Dombois, Eugen M. 'Lute Temperament in Hans Gerle (1532).' *The Lute* 22 (1982) 3–13

Elders *Studien*   Elders, Willem. *Studien zur Symbolik in der Musik der Alten Niederländer*. Bilthoven 1968

Ellsworth *Berkeley*   Ellsworth, Oliver B. *The Berkeley Manuscript*. Lincoln 1984

Ellsworth *Origin*   — 'The Origin of the Coniuncta: A Reappraisal.' JMT 17 (1973) 86–109

Eubank *Spanish*   Eubank, Lee E. 'Spanish Intabulations in the Sixteenth Century.' PHD diss, Indiana University 1974

Fenlon MMEME   Fenlon, Iain, ed. *Music in Medieval and Early Modern Europe: Patronage, Sources, and Texts*. Cambridge 1981

Finscher *Formen*   Finscher, Ludwig, ed. *Formen und Probleme der Überlieferung mehrstimmiger Musik im Zeitalter Josquins Desprez*. Munich 1981

Fox *Accidentals*   Fox, Charles Warren, 'Accidentals in Vihuela Tablatures.' BAMS 4 (1938) 22–4

Garcia *Cerone*   Garcia, Francisco. 'Pietro Cerone's *El Melopeo y Maestro*: A Synthesis of Sixteenth-Century Musical Theory.' PHD diss, Northwestern University 1978

Glixon *Lutenists*   Glixon, Jonathon. 'Lutenists in Renaissance Venice: Some Notes from the Archives.' JLSA 16 (1983) 15–26

Godt *Comments*   Godt, Irving. 'Comments and Issues.' *JAMS* 31 (1978) 385–8

Godt *Lesson*   — 'A Lesson in *Musica Ficta* from Guillaume Costeley and Le Roy & Ballard, 1570–1579.' *MR* 38 (1977) 159–62

Godt *Motivic*   — 'Motivic Integration in Josquin's Motets.' *JMT* 21 (1977) 264–92

Haar *False*   Haar, James. 'False Relations and Chromaticism in Sixteenth-Century Music.' *JAMS* 30 (1977) 391–418

Haar *Hexachord*   — 'A Sixteenth-Century Hexachord Composition.' *JMT* 19 (1975) 32–45

Haar *Zarlino*   'Zarlino's Definition of Fugue and Imitation.' *JAMS* 24 (1971) 226–54

Hanen *Escorial*   Hanen, Martha K. *The Chansonnier El Escorial IV. a.24.* 3 vols. Henryville, Pa. 1983

Harden *Musica*   Harden, Jean. '"Musica Ficta" in Machaut.' *EM* 5 (1977) 473–7

Harden *Machaut*   — 'Sharps, Flats, and Scribes: *Musica Ficta* in the Machaut Manuscripts.' PHD diss, Cornell University 1983

Harrán *Comments*   Harrán, Don. 'Comments and Issues.' *JAMS* 31 (1978) 388–95

Harrán *More*   — 'More Evidence for Cautionary Signs.' *JAMS* 31 (1978) 490–4

Harrán *New*   — 'New Evidence for Musica Ficta: The Cautionary Sign.' *JAMS* 29 (1976) 77–98

Harwood *Le Roy*   Harwood, Ian. 'On the Publication of Adrian Le Roy's Lute Instructions.' *LSJ* 18 (1976) 30–6

Heck *Lute*   Heck, Thomas F. 'Lute Music: Tablatures, Textures, and Transcriptions.' *JLSA* 7 (1974) 19–30

Henderson *Solmization*   Henderson, Robert Vladimir. 'Solmization Syllables in Musical Theory, 1100 to 1600.' PHD diss, Columbia University 1969

Henning *Virdung*   Henning, Uta. 'The Lute Made Easy: A Chapter from Virdung's *Musica getutscht* (1511).' *LSJ* 15 (1973) 20–36

Herlinger *Marchetto*   Herlinger, Jan W. *The Lucidarium of Marchetto of Padua.* Chicago 1985

Honegger *Tablature*   Honegger, Marc. 'La Tablature de D. Pisador et le problème des altérations au XVIe siècle.' *RM* 59 (1973) 38–59 and 191–230; 60 (1974) 3–32

Honegger *Pisador*   — 'Les Messes de Josquin des Prés dans la tablature de Diego Pisador (Salamanque 1552): Contribution à l'étude des altérations au XVIe siècle.' PHD diss, University of Paris 1970

Hoppin *Conflicting*   Hoppin, Richard H. 'Conflicting Signatures Reviewed.' *JAMS* 9 (1956) 97–117

Hoppin *Partial*   — 'Partial Signatures and Musica Ficta in Some Early 15th-Century Sources.' *JAMS* 6 (1953) 197–215

Howell *Pareja*   Howell, Standley. 'Ramos de Pareja's "Brief Discussion of Various Instruments."' *JAMIS* 11 (1985) 14–37

Howlett *Agricola*   Howlett, Derq. "A Translation of Three Treatises by Martin Agricola." PHD diss, Ohio State University 1979

Hughes *Ficta*   Hughes, Andrew. *Manuscript Accidentals: Ficta in Focus 1350–1450*. MSD 27. Np 1972

Hughes *Review*   — Review of *The Theory of Hexachords, Solmization, and the Modal System* by Gaston G. Allaire (MSD 24, 1972). *JAMS* 27 (1974) 132–9

Hughes *Ugolino*   — 'Ugolino: The Monochord and Musica Ficta.' *MD* 23 (1969) 21–39

Hughes & Bent *Old Hall*   Hughes, Andrew, and Margaret Bent, eds. *The Old Hall Manuscript*. CMM 46. Np 1969

Hultberg *Pisador*   Hultberg, Warren E. 'Diego Pisador's *Libro de Música de Vihuela* (1552).' In *Festival Essays for Pauline Alderman* ed Burton L. Karson (Provo, Utah 1976) 29–51

Jacobs *Correa*   Jacobs, Charles. *Francisco Correa de Arauxo*. The Hague 1973

Jacobs *Milán*   — *Luis de Milán, El Maestro*. London 1971

Jacobs *Fuenllana*   — *Miguel de Fuenllana, Orphenica lyra*. Oxford 1978

Jacobs *Performance*   — 'The Performance Practice of Spanish Renaissance Keyboard Music.' PHD diss, New York University 1962

Jacobs *Ficta*   — 'Spanish Renaissance Discussion of Musica Ficta.' *PAPS* 112 (1968) 277–98

Jacobs *Notation*   — *Tempo Notation in Renaissance Spain*. New York 1964

Jacobs *Transcription*   — 'The Transcription Technique and Style of Antonio de Cabezón as Shown in His Thirteen Intabulations of Music by Josquin des Prez.' MA thesis, New York University 1957

Janssen *Waytes*   Janssen, Carole Ann. 'The Waytes of Norwich in Medieval and Renaissance Civic Pageantry.' PHD diss, University of New Brunswick 1978

Judd *Analysis*   Judd, Cristle Collins. 'Some Problems of Pre-
                         Baroque Analysis: An Examination of Josquin's
                         Ave Maria ... Virgo Serena.' MA 4 (1985) 201–39
Kastner MME 6   Kastner, Santiago, ed. *Francisco Correa de Arauxo,
                         Libro de Tientos ... Facultad Orgánica* (Alcala 1626).
                         Monumentos de la música española, vol 6.
                         Barcelona 1948
Kemp NDW   Kemp, William. *Kemp's nine daies wonder* (London
                         1600). Ed Alexander Dyce. London 1840
Kirby *Finck*   Kirby, Frank E. 'Hermann Finck's *Practica Musica*: A
                         Comparative Study in Sixteenth-Century German
                         Musical Theory.' PHD diss, Yale University 1957
Kottick *Flats*   Kottick, Edward L. 'Flats, Modality, Musica Ficta in
                         Some Early Renaissance Chansons.' *JMT* 12 (1968)
                         264–80
Lampl *Praetorius*   Lampl, Hans. 'A Translation of *Syntagma Musicum* III
                         by Michael Praetorius.' DMA diss, University of
                         Southern California 1957
Lee *Lanfranco*   Lee, Barbara. 'Giovanni Maria Lanfranco's *Scintille di
                         musica* and Its Relation to 16th-Century Music
                         Theory.' PHD diss, Cornell University 1961
Levy *Costeley*   Levy, Kenneth. 'Costeley's Chromatic Chanson.'
                         AnM 3 (1955) 213–63
Lindley *Milán*   Lindley, Mark. 'Luis Milán and Meantone Tempera-
                         ment.' *JLSA* 11 (1978) 45–62
Lindley *Temperaments*   — *Lutes, Viols, and Temperaments.* Cambridge 1984
Lockwood *Dispute*   Lockwood, Lewis. 'A Dispute on Accidentals in Six-
                         teenth-Century Rome.' *AM* 2 (1965) 24–40
Lockwood *Sample*   'A Sample Problem of *Musica Ficta*: Willaert's *Pater
                         Noster.*' In *Studies in Music History*: *Essays for Oliver
                         Strunk* ed Harold Powers (Princeton 1968) 161–
                         82
Lowinsky *Accidentals*   Lowinsky, Edward E. 'Accidentals (musica ficta).' *TVNM*
                         24 (1974) 53–69
Lowinsky *Willaert*   — 'Adrian Willaert's Chromatic "Duo" Re-examined.'
                         TVNM 18 (1956) 1–36
Lowinsky *Conflicting*   — 'Conflicting Views on Conflicting Signatures.' *JAMS*
                         7 (1954) 181–204
Lowinsky *Early*   — 'Early Scores in Manuscript.' *JAMS* 13 (1960) 126–73
Lowinsky *Echoes*   — 'Echoes of Adrian Willaert's Chromatic "Duo" in
                         Sixteenth and Seventeenth-Century Compositions.'
                         In *Studies in Music History*: *Essays for Oliver Strunk* ed
                         Harold Powers (Princeton 1968) 183–238

Lowinsky *Musica Nova* — Foreword to *Musica Nova* ed H. Colin Slim (Chicago 1964) v–xxi

Lowinsky *Function* — 'The Function of Conflicting Signatures in Early Polyphonic Music.' MQ 31 (1945) 227–60

Lowinsky *Goddess* — 'The Goddess Fortuna in Music.' MQ 29 (1943) 45–77

Lowinsky *Ascanio* — 'Josquin des Prez and Ascanio Sforza.' In *Il Duomo di Milano, Congresso internazionale, Atti*, vol 2, ed Maria Luisa Gatti Perer (Milan 1969) 17–22

Lowinsky *Greiter* — 'Matthaeus Greiter's *Fortuna*: An Experiment in Chromaticism and in Musical Iconography.' MQ 42 (1956) 500–19 and 43 (1957) 68–85

Lowinsky *Scores* — 'On the Use of Scores by Sixteenth-Century Musicians.' JAMS 1 (1948) 17–23

Lowinsky *Secret* — *Secret Chromatic Art in the Netherlands Motet*. New York 1946

Lowinsky *Re-examined* — 'Secret Chromatic Art *Re-examined*.' In Brook *Perspectives* pp 91–135

Lowinsky *Tonality* — *Tonality and Atonality in Sixteenth-Century Music*. Berkeley, Calif 1961

Lowinsky *Josquin* — ed. *Josquin des Prez*. London 1976

MacClintock *Fronimo* — MacClintock, Carol. *Vincenzo Galilei, Fronimo 1584*. MSD 39. Neuhausen-Stuttgart 1985

McGary *Escorial* — McGary, Thomas J. 'Partial Signature Implications in the Escorial Manuscript V.III. 24' MR 40 (1979) 77–89

Marco & Palisca *Art* — Marco, Guy A., and Claude V. Palisca. *The Art of Counterpoint*. New Haven 1968

Marx *Tabulaturen* — Marx, Hans Joachim. *Tabulaturen des XVI. Jahhunderts*, Teil 1. Basel 1967

Meier *Reservata* — Meier, Bernhard. 'The Musica Reservata of Adrianus Petit Coclico and Its Relationship to Josquin.' MD 10 (1956) 67–105

Meier *Modes* — *The Modes of Classical Vocal Polyphony*. Trans Ellen S. Beebe. New York 1988

Miller *Gaffurius* — Miller, Clement A., trans. *Franchinus Gaffurius, Practica Musicae*. MSD 20. Np 1968

Miller *Glarean* — trans. *Heinrich Glarean, Dodecachordon*. MSD 6. Np 1965

Miller *Cardanus* — trans. *Hieronymous Cardanus (1501–1576): Writings on Music*. MSD 32. Np 1973

Miller *Cochlaeus* — trans. *Johannes Cochlaeus, Tetrachordum musices*. MSD 23. Np 1970

Miller *Burtius*	— trans. *Nicolaus Burtius, Musices opusculum*. MSD 37. Neuhausen-Stuttgart 1983
Miller *Heyden*	— trans. *Sebald Heyden, De arte canendi*. MSD 26. Np 1972 'Musica ficta.' *New Grove* 12: 802–11
Ness *Francesco*	Ness, Arthur J. *The Lute Music of Francesco Canova da Milano* (1497–1543). Cambridge, Mass 1970
New Grove	*The New Grove Dictionary of Music and Musicians*. 20 vols. Ed Stanley Sadie. London 1980
Noblitt *Chromatic*	Noblitt, Thomas. 'Chromatic Cross-Relations and Editorial *Musica Ficta* in Masses of Obrecht.' TVNM 32 (1982) 30–44
Noblitt *Textual*	— 'Textual Criticism of Selected Works Published by Petrucci.' In Finscher *Formen* pp 201–44
Novack *Tonal*	Novack, Saul. 'Tonal Tendencies in Josquin's Use of Harmony.' In Lowinsky *Josquin* pp 317–33
Osthoff *Josquin*	Osthoff, Helmuth. *Josquin Desprez*. 2 vols. Tutzing 1962–5
Palisca *Rhetorical*	Palisca, Claude V. '*Ut Oratoria Musica*: The Rhetorical Basis of Musical Mannerism.' In *The Meaning of Mannerism* ed Franklin W. Robinson and Stephen G. Nichols (Hanover NH 1972) 37–65
Parrish *Manual*	Parrish, Carl. 'A Renaissance Music Manual for Choirboys.' In *Aspects of Medieval and Renaissance Music* ed Jan La Rue (New York 1966) 649–64
Perkins *Mode*	Perkins, Leeman L. 'Mode and Structure in the Masses of Josquin.' JAMS 26 (1973) 189–239
Perkins & Garey *Mellon*	Perkins, Leeman L., and Howard Garey. *The Mellon Chansonnier*. 2 vols. New Haven 1979
Pesce *Affinities*	Pesce, Dolores. *The Affinities and Medieval Transposition*. Bloomington 1987
Pesce *Transposition*	— 'B-flat: Transposition or Transformation?' JM 4 (1985–6) 330–49
Pierce *Gerle*	Pierce, Jane I. 'Hans Gerle: Sixteenth-Century Lutenist and Pedagogue.' PHD diss, University of North Carolina 1973
Pogue *Editor*	Pogue, Samuel F. 'A Sixteenth-Century Editor at Work: Gardane and Moderne.' JM 1 (1982) 217–38
Pope *Vihuela*	Pope, Isabel. 'La vihuela y su música en el ambiente humanístico.' NRFH 15 (1961) 364–76
Powers *Tonal*	Powers, Harold S. 'Tonal Types and Modal Categories in Renaissance Polyphony.' JAMS 34 (1981) 428–70
Prizer *Lutenists*	Prizer, William F. 'Lutenists at the Court of Mantua in

	the Late Fifteenth and Early Sixteenth Centuries.' *JLSA* 13 (1980) 5–34
Routley *Guide*	Routley, Nicholas. 'A Practical Guide to *Musica Ficta*.' *EM* 13 (1985) 59–71
Rubenstein *Woltz*	Rubenstein, Marion H. 'Johann Woltz: *Nova musices organicae tabulatura*: A Critical Study and Partial Transcription.' MMUS thesis, King's College, University of London 1976
Rubio *Polyphony*	Rubio, P. Samuel. *Classical Polyphony*. Trans Thomas Rive. Oxford 1972
Samuel *Modality*	Samuel, Rhian. 'Modality, Tonality, and *Musica Ficta* in the Sixteenth-Century Chanson.' PHD diss, Washington University 1978
Schmidt *Spinacino*	Schmidt, Henry L. 'The First Printed Lute Books: Francesco Spinacino's *Intabulatura de Lauto, Libro Primo and Libro Secondo* (Venice: Petrucci 1507).' PHD diss, University of North Carolina 1969
Schmidt-Görg *Gombert*	Schmidt-Görg, Joseph. *Nicholas Gombert, Collected Works*. CMM 6. Np 1951–75
Seay *Coniuncta*	Seay, Albert. 'The 15th-Century *Coniuncta*: A Preliminary Survey.' In *Aspects of Medieval and Renaissance Music* ed Jan La Rue (New York 1966) 723–37
Seay *Hothby*	— 'Hothby, John.' *New Grove* 8:729–30
Seay *Tinctoris 1*	— *Johannes Tinctoris, Opera Theoretica* I. CSM 22. Np 1975
Seay *Tinctoris 2*	— *Johannes Tinctoris, Opera Theoretica* II. CSM 22. Np 1975
Seay *Martínez*	— ed. *Goncalo Martínez de Biscargui, Arte de Canto Llano*. Colorado Springs 1979
Seay *Coclico*	— trans. *Adrian Petit Coclico, Musical Compendium*. Colorado Springs 1973
Seay *Tinctoris/Tones*	— trans. *Johannes Tinctoris, Concerning the Nature and Propriety of Tones*. Colorado Springs 1976
Seay *Tinctoris/ Counterpoint*	— trans. *Johannes Tinctoris, The Art of Counterpoint*. MSD 5. Np 1961
Seay *Listenius*	— trans. *Nicolaus Listenius, Music*. Colorado Springs 1975
Slim *Francesco*	Slim, H. Colin. 'Francesco da Milano (1497–1543/44).' *MD* 18 (1964) 63–84 and 19 (1965) 109–28
Slim *Versions*	— 'Instrumental Versions, c. 1515–1544, of a Late-Fifteenth-Century Flemish Chanson, *O waerde mont*.' In Fenlon *MMEME* pp 131–61

Smijers *Werken*   Smijers, Albert, et al, eds. *Werken van Josquin des Prez*. Amsterdam 1921–69

Smith *Waissel*   Smith, Douglas Alton. 'The Instructions in Matthaeus Waissel's Lautenbuch.' *JLSA* 8 (1975) 49–79

Smith *Accidentalism*   Smith, F.J. '"Accidentalism" in Fourteenth-Century Music.' *RBM* 24 (1970) 42–51

Snow *Ceballos*   Snow, Robert J. *The Extant Music of Rodrigo de Ceballos and Its Sources*. Detroit 1980
'Solmization' *New Grove* 17: 458–62

Sonnino *Handbook*   Sonnino, Lee A. *A Handbook to Sixteenth-Century Rhetoric*. London 1968

Southard *Newsidler*   Southard, Marc, and Suzana Cooper. 'A Translation of Hans Newsidler's *Ein Newgeordent Künstlich Lautenbuch* ... (*1536*).' *JLSA* 11 (1978) 5–25

Sovik *Theorists*   Sovik, Thomas Paul. 'Music Theorists of the Bohemian Reformation: Translation and Critique of the Treatises of Jan Blahoslav and Jan Josquin.' PHD diss, Ohio State University 1985

Spencer *Board*   Spencer, Robert, ed. *The Board Lute Book*. Leeds 1976

Stevenson *Bermudo*   Stevenson, Robert. *Juan Bermudo*. The Hague 1960

Tischler *Ficta*   Tischler, Hans. '"Musica Ficta" in the Thirteenth Century.' *ML* 54 (1973) 38–56

Toft *Approach*   Toft, Robert. 'An Approach to Performing the Mid 16th-Century Italian Lute Fantasia.' *The Lute* 25 (1985) 3–16

Toft *Absalon*   — 'Pitch Content and Modal Procedure in Josquin's *Absalon, fili mi*' *TVNM* 33 (1983) 3–27

Toft *Pitch*   — 'Pitch Content and Modal Procedure in Selected Motets of Josquin Desprez: A Comparative Study of the Printed Intabulations with the Vocal Sources.' PHD diss, King's College, University of London 1983

Toft *Traditions*   — 'Traditions of Pitch Content in the Sources of Two Sixteenth-Century Motets.' *ML* 69 (1988) 334–44

Tomlinson *Culture*   Tomlinson, Gary. 'The Web of Culture: A Context for Musicology.' *19th-Century Music* 7 (1984) 350–62

Unger *Rhetoric*   Unger, Hans-Heinrich. *Die Beziehungen zwischen Musik und Rhetoric im 16.–18. Jahrhundert*. Würzburg 1941; repr Hildesheim 1982

Urquhart *Montanos*   Urquhart, Dan Murdock. 'Francisco de Montanos's *Arte de Música Theórica y Prática*: A Translation and

Commentary.' PHD diss, University of Rochester 1969

Vaccaro *Luth* Vaccaro, Jean-Michel. *La Musique de luth en France au XVIe siècle*. Paris 1981

Vaccaro *Rippe* — ed. *Œuvres d'Albert de Rippe*. Paris 1972

Vogel *Wheel* Vogel, Roger C. 'The Musical Wheel of Domingo Marcos Durán.' CMS 22 (1982) 51–66

Vogel *Durán* — 'The Theoretical Writings of Domingo Marcos Durán: A Translation and Commentary.' PHD diss, Ohio State University 1975

Warburton *Sicher* Warburton, Thomas. 'Fridolin Sicher's Tablature: A Guide to Keyboard Performance of Vocal Music.' PHD diss, University of Michigan 1969

Warburton *Josquin* — ed. *Keyboard Intabulations of Music by Josquin des Prez*. Madison, Wisc 1980

Ward *Editorial* Ward, John. 'The Editorial Methods of Venegas de Henestrosa.' MD 6 (1952) 105–13

Ward *Borrowed* — 'The Use of Borrowed Material in 16th-Century Instrumental Music.' JAMS 5 (1952) 88–98

Ward *Vihuela* — 'The Vihuela de Mano and Its Music (1536–1576).' PHD diss, New York University 1953

Ware *Dissonance* Ware, John Marley. 'Dissonance Treatment in Sacred Vocal Polyphony in More than Five Parts up to the Death of Josquin des Prez (1521).' PHD diss, Louisiana State University 1978

Wienandt *Francesco* Wienandt, Elwyn A. 'Musical Style in the Lute Compositions of Francesco da Milano (1498–1543).' PHD diss, University of Iowa 1951

Yong *Inventory* Yong, Kwee Him. 'Sixteenth-Century Printed Instrumental Arrangements of Works by Josquin des Prez: An Inventory.' TVNM 22 (1971–2) 43–66

Zager *Solmization* Zager, Daniel. 'From the Singer's Point of View: A Case Study in Hexachordal Solmization as a Guide to *Musica Recta* and *Musica Ficta* in Fifteenth-Century Vocal Music.' CM 43 (1987) 7–21

LIST OF EXAMPLES

(c) 'In exitu' I 134–5 (Ochsenkun 1558)
(d) 'Benedicta es' I 83–5 (♮♯ Teghi 1547, Fuenllana 1554, and
Ochsenkun 1558; ♮♯ Phalèse 1553 and Cabezón 1578; ♯♯ Gintzler 1547,
Rippe 1558, and M. Newsidler 1574)

2.43   (a) 'In exitu' II 57–9 (Ochsenkun 1558)
        (b) 'Memor esto' I 44–6 (H. Newsidler 1536)
2.44   (a) 'Praeter rerum' I 61–2 (Fuenllana 1554)
        (b) 'In exitu' I 67–8 (Ochsenkun 1558)
2.45   'Qui habitat' I 97–9 (Ochsenkun 1558)
2.46   'Benedicta es' I 64–5
2.47   Lupi 'Benedictus dominus' I 21–3 (Gintzler 1547)
2.48   (a) 'Inviolata' I 20–1 (Gerle 1533 and Valderrávano 1547)
        (b) 'Qui habitat' I 41 (Gerle 1533)
2.49   'Qui habitat' I 89–90 (Gerle 1533)
2.50   (a) 'Qui habitat' I 105–9 (Gerle 1533, Ochsenkun 1558, and Bakfark 1565)
        (b) 'Stabat Mater' I 33–4 (Milano before 1536, Gintzler 1547, Phalèse 1553,
        Ochsenkun 1558, and Cabezón 1578)
2.51   'Pater noster' II 67–8
2.52   'In exitu' III 106–8 (Ochsenkun 1558)
2.53   'Praeter rerum' I 58–60 (Rippe 1555 and Ochsenkun 1558)
2.54   *Second livre* ..., 'Pavane' (F♯ Gervaise 1547; B♭ Hessen 1555)
2.55   (a) 'Memor esto' I 112–13 (H. Newsidler 1536)
        (b) 'Ave Maria' 33–5 (Spinacino 1507)
2.56   'Pater noster' II 49–51 (♮ Milano 1546, Valderrávano 1547,
        Ochsenkun 1558, and Cabezón 1578; ♭ Gintzler 1547 and Teghi 1547)
2.57   'Qui habitat' I 32–7 (*fuga* – Ochsenkun 1558 and Bakfark 1565;
        imitatione – Gerle 1533)
2.58   'Inviolata' I 52–6 (Cabezón 1578)
2.59   'Pater noster' II 46–9
2.60   (a) 'Stabat Mater' I 1–2 (Milano before 1536)
        (b) 'Pater noster' I 1–4 (Ochsenkun 1558)
2.61   'Stabat Mater' II 56 (Ochsenkun 1558)
2.62   (a) 'Pater noster' I 4 (Milano 1546)
        (b) 'Stabat Mater' I 74–5 (Ochsenkun 1558)

CHAPTER 3

3.1   (a) Eckel 'Gesell, wis Urlaub' 7–9 (Gerle 1546, for lute)
        (b) Senfl 'Mein selbs bin ich' 19–21 (Gerle 1532, for viols)
3.2   Senfl 'Patientiam muess ich han' 20–1 (Gerle 1532, for viols and for lute)
3.3   Lupi 'Spes salutis' I 19–21 (Gerle 1546, for lute)
3.4   Senfl 'O Herr, ich rüef dein'n Namen an' (Gerle 1546, for viols)
3.5   Lupi 'Spes salutis' I 24–8 (Gerle 1546, for lute)
3.6   Lupi 'Spes salutis' II 21–3 (Gerle 1546, for lute)

INDEX OF NAMES
AND TITLES

References to musical examples are in boldface type.

GENERAL INDEX

ascending lines, treatment of 90–2

b durum. See sharps and flats
b mollis. See sharps and flats

cadence. *See clausula*
canon 88–9, 123–4
causa pulchritudinis 126
chain-reaction 158n29, 161n5
chromaticism. *See clausula*, chromaticism at. *See also* secret chromatic art
chronological trends 5
clausula: approaches to, 17–23, 45–71,
    88–9, 119, 121–2, 128, 129, 130,
    153n12, 157n21; chromaticism at,
    22–3, 56–62, 70, 130, 156n15;
    function of within mode, 46–9, 51,
    62, 152n9; preclusion of subsemitone
    at, 20–1, 22–3, 48, 50–6, 98, 119,
    121–2, 123, 157n16; raised thirds at,
    23–4, 70–1, 85, 122–3, 157n25; 6–5–
    1 formula at, 65–70, 122;
    subsemitone at, 17–23, 46–7, 48, 62–
    5, 88, 92, 96–9, 119, 121–2, 128, 129,
    130, 152n9, 153n14, 157nn21, 25;
    subsemitone omitted at, 48–50;

subtone at, 46–50, 63, 65, 96–9, 121–
    2, 152n9; suprasemitone at, 17, 19,
    21–2, 46–7, 48, 62–5, 89, 99, 105,
    119, 121–2, 152n9, 157n21; types
    (avoided, imperfect, interrupted,
    perfect), 16, 153n12
cláusula disimulada 37
cláusula hurtada 28
climax 114, 115, 162n16, 163n17
code-note 161n5
compás 28
composers, intentions of 3, 6, 45, 131,
    151n2
coniuncta 26
contextual approaches to musicology 4,
    99–102, 131–3, 154nn34, 36, 160n39
counterpoint 10
cross relations. *See* dissonance,
    nonharmonic relations

deductio 14, 126, 128
descending lines, treatment of 90–2
diesis 121, 157n25, 160n39
dissonance: at cadences, 20–3, 48, 50,
    65; in octaves, 10, 30–2, 44, 80–2,
    110–11, 128, 130, 154n34, 159nn35–